Managing Strategic and Capital Investment Decisions

Going Beyond the Numbers to Improve Decision Making

Thomas Klammer
University of North Texas
for the Cost Management System Program
of the Consortium for Advanced Manufacturing-International

A project undertaken by the
Institute of Management Accountants
Montvale, New Jersey
Consortium for Advanced Manufacturing-International

IRWIN
Professional Publishing

Burr Ridge, IL 60521
New York, NY 10001

Senior editor: Michael E. Desposito
Project editor: Jane Lightell
Assistant production manager: Jon Christopher
Printer: Book Press, Inc.

Library of Congress Cataloging-in-Publication Data

Klammer, Thomas P., 1944-
    Managing strategic and capital investment decisions : going beyond the numbers to improve decision making / Thomas Klammer.
      p.   cm.
    Includes bibliographical references.
    ISBN 0-7863-0112-0
    1. Capital investments—United States—Decision making.
    2. Investments—United States. I. Title.
    HG4028 . C4K486 1994
    658 . 15'54—dc20   93-5290

Printed in the United States of America

1 2 3 4 5 6 7 8 9 0 BP 0 9 8 7 6 5 4 3

Meeting the Challenge

During the past decade, management has been obsessed with improvement—and rightly so. Many philosophies and techniques have surfaced hoping to lead organizations to a safe haven from their competition.

The reality of life has proved that there is no one magic formula that will save the day. There is, however, the possibility of improvement that exists through constantly challenging what works today, knowing it well may fall short tomorrow.

Since the inception of the Cost Management System (CMS) Program of CAM-I, program members from various companies and industries have recognized the need to improve the investment management process. To meet this need, the investment management work group was formed. Understanding the extensive changes taking place in industry, the group strongly voiced the need to rethink the investment process. Previous methods and criteria for decision making may prove misleading or even disastrous in today's business environment.

This book is a collection of the ideas and experiences of the members of the work group. Several research projects sponsored by the CMS Program also have provided substantial data presented in this document. This material has been published previously by CAM-I CMS to help organizations identify opportunities for improving their investment management process.

The program would like to recognize the considerable effort the members of the investment management work group devoted to this project and specifically thank the Institute of Management Accountants for its enthusiastic encouragement and support.

Peter A. Zampino
Director
CAM-I Advanced Management Programs

Foreword

Managing Strategic and Capital Investment Decisions: Going Beyond the Numbers to Improve Decision Making offers a fresh perspective on the way investments are managed. The centerpiece of the study is the investment management matrix. The matrix provides a functional approach to continuously improving the investment management process.

The findings in this guide complement a previously published IMA research study, *The Capital Expenditure Decision*, released in 1983. The concepts developed by CAM-I's Cost Management System interest group fill an existing void. IMA is proud to bring this valuable guide to the management accounting profession.

IMA recognizes the dedication of CAM-I's interest group and of two members who also serve on IMA national committees—Thomas Klammer (Committee on Academic Relations) and Paul P. Danesi, Jr. (Committee on Research). We are indebted to the chairman of the interest group, Frank Reynolds (Eastman Kodak); to Peter Zampino, director of Advanced Management Programs, CAM-I; and to IMA's Committee on Research for making this guide possible.

The report reflects the views of the Cost Management System interest group and not necessarily those of the Institute or the Committee on Research.

Julian Freedman
Director of Research
Institute of Management Accountants

Preface

An effective management system helps a company's leaders make informed strategic, tactical, and operating decisions about resource acquisition and use. Investment management is the process used to identify and analyze opportunities that can improve the performance of the firm. Investment opportunities include traditional capital expenditures for plant (facilities), people, and technology. They also include activities such as managing the firm's capital structure, ranking acquisition and disposition prospects, analyzing research and development opportunities, and examining major marketing efforts.

An effective investment management process helps the firm reach its strategic goals using the optimal amount of limited resources. The principles and procedures of investment management that are summarized in this guide apply to any organization and any type of investment. These ideas can help you identify opportunities for improving your firm's investment management process.

The concepts and tools described apply to a broad range of investments. You probably will apply these ideas initially in capital investment decisions, so we use capital investment to illustrate them. The emphasis is on the importance of creating linkages. You need linkage across the investment management process steps. You also need linkage between these steps and the complexity level of the firm or the investment.

A changing business environment makes improving the investment management process essential. Global competition, a total quality emphasis, increased flexibility, and continuous improvement goals require restructuring of investment management practices. The process is one part of the total management system. Budgeting, performance measurement, internal control, and special project analysis are other integral parts of the system. All segments should work together.

Are these elements properly coordinated in your company? Would changes in the investment decision process offer an opportunity to improve the coordination?

The goal of investment management is to attain strategic objectives. A company makes investments in technology, equipment, people, systems, and related resources. The system should help the firm identify resources and start activities that will improve performance. Enhancements in the process can provide significant benefits for the firm's stakeholders—shareholders, management, employees, customers, and local communities.

Are you interested in or responsible for developing or changing the investment management process? If so, you should find this guide a useful tool. It will help you identify opportunities for change.

- Basic investment management issues are identified and described throughout the text.

- The book provides guidance for assessing your investment management capabilities.

- Tools and technologies for performing investment management are described. These tools illustrate the process.

The principles and procedures are extensions of ideas that were articulated in the original CAM-I conceptual design.[1] CAM-I research added to these concepts. This guide provides a summary of the major findings of these research studies. It will help you to evaluate and change your firm's investment management practices.

This is not a "how to do" investment management text. We do provide a series of exhibits and short examples, which explain the basic investment management concepts. They allow you to relate these ideas to situations faced by your company.

Later publications will provide more detailed descriptions and explanations of specific practices and techniques. They will include a detailed literature summary tied to the cells of the investment management matrix discussed throughout this book. There is also a summary article, "Improving Investment Decisions," in the July 1993 issue of *Management Accounting*, the official magazine of the Institute of Management Accountants.

We are interested in your reactions, suggestions, and comments about the ideas included in this guide. We would especially welcome examples and illustrations related to any part of the investment management decision process. Please direct your correspondence to:

Professor Thomas Klammer
College of Business Administration
Department of Accounting
University of North Texas
P.O. Box 13677
Denton, TX 76203-3677

Telephone: (817) 565-3099   Fax: (817) 565-3803

---

[1]Published as *Cost Management for Today's Advanced Manufacturing—The CAM-I Conceptual Design*, edited by Callie Berliner and James A. Brimson, Harvard Business School Press, Boston, 1988.

Acknowledgments

The investment management interest group responsible for this guide is part of the Cost Management System (CMS) Program of CAM-I (Consortium for Advanced Manufacturing-International). The group's mission is to develop usable investment management methods that will help firms reach their strategic goals. The purpose of the guide is to help companies understand and use ideas inherent in the CMS conceptual design.

The interest group, through the CMS Program, sponsored research, testing, and analysis of the investment management matrix. Extensive work has been done on the tools described in this guide, and this effort is continuing. The group believes that the suggested principles and procedures can improve a company's investment management process.

The guide uses the findings of the research sponsored by the interest group and the CMS Program. Contributions from this research can be found throughout the text. Parts of the guide also are the direct result of work by various members of the CMS investment management group.

Group members who contributed extensively to the guide include:

Steve Andreou	General Motors
Adam Cywar	IBM
Paul P. Danesi, Jr.	Texas Instruments

Scott Hoesterey	Northrup
Thomas Klammer	University of North Texas
Frank Reynolds	Eastman Kodak
Betsy See	Texas Instruments
Kelly Schjenken	McDonnell Douglas
Sam Shafer	Procter & Gamble
Lew Soloway	Cost Management Strategies
Bob Wurzelbacher	Procter & Gamble
Rande Wagner	General Dynamics

Other interest group members also gave generously of their time and talent at various CMS meetings.

About the Author

Thomas Klammer, Ph.D., CPA, is a Regent's Professor of Accounting at the University of North Texas. He has extensive experience in accounting education with both university students and practicing accounting professionals through continuing education programs.

He has served on numerous professional and academic committees and is a past president of the Management Accounting Section of the American Accounting Association. Dr. Klammer currently is a member of the IMA Committee on Academic Relations and CAM-I's Investment Management Committee. He also is working actively with CAM-I on several projects.

Dr. Klammer has published extensively in the practice and academic literature. His work includes books and more than 20 articles. His research has centered on how capital investments are made and the presentation of cash flow information. Dr. Klammer is also the author of nationally used training materials on cash flow, financial instruments, and capital budgeting.

Dr. Klammer earned his Ph.D. degree from the University of Wisconsin and BBA and MBA degrees from Western Michigan University.

Table of Contents

Managing Strategic and Capital Investment Decisions

Chapter 1

Overview of Investment Management

An effective management system helps a company use resources to produce products or services competitive in cost, time, quality, and functionality. Identifying and evaluating investment opportunities that improve performance in these areas are key parts of this system. *Investment management* is identifying and evaluating technology, equipment, people, systems, and related opportunities that improve performance. Operationally, investment management is an extension of the capital investment process. It emphasizes decisions that add value to the company and benefit its stakeholders.

The investment management process is important. It helps management identify opportunities and analyze alternatives. Perceived problems with investment management caused the Cost Management Systems (CMS) program of CAM-I (Consortium for Advanced Manufacturing-International) to research the process.

The result was a CMS investment management framework that includes four major parts:

1. Part one explains the guiding principles of investment management.
2. Part two describes the investment management core process steps.

3. Part three reviews the levels of investment management complexity and evolution through these levels.
4. Part four explains selected investment management tools and technologies.

This book discusses the guiding principles first and then explains the core processes. It examines the complexity levels and the developmental progression within each step and describes selected tools. It includes concepts, ideas, and examples you can use in your company. With the investment management framework you can analyze and improve your company's investment management practices. The guide helps in other ways:

•   It explains the basic assumptions, the guiding principles of investment management. It shows how these principles relate to investment management problems.

•   The text identifies and illustrates concepts, principles, and systems that can improve overall investment management.

•   Sections show how and why techniques and tools vary with the level of organizational complexity and with the nature of the investment decision.

•   The guide defines and illustrates tools for investment analysis that involve multiple decision criteria.

A model, the investment management matrix, shows the concepts, principles, and applications of the investment management process. The matrix has a conceptual focus because implementation approaches vary by type of firm and with the investment decision. If you understand the matrix you can adapt and use the ideas.

The following assumptions about the investment management environment influence the information that is discussed and illustrated in this guide:

- There are opportunities to improve existing investment management processes.

- Workable general methods for exploiting these opportunities exist.

- The investment management matrix provides a functional approach that can be used for continuously improving the investment management process.

- Implementation of investment management concepts, principles, and system methodology is evolutionary. The company's level(s) of organizational complexity and the investment complexity influence the process.

Guiding Principles

Effective investment management systems take many forms. They use varied procedures and functionally different terminology. Five guiding principles are central to the process. A list of these principles appears in Exhibit 1-1, and a brief explanation is given below. How a company satisfies each of the principles varies with the product, market, location, and organizational complexity of the firm.

Principle 1. Relate investment decisions to the strategic plans and operating goals of the company. Set up performance measures that compare the results of the decision with the company's strategies.

Exhibit 1-1. GUIDING PRINCIPLES

1. Relate investment decisions to the strategic plans and operating goals of the company. Set up performance measures that compare the results of the decision with the company's strategies.

2. Evaluate the investment alternatives consistently.

3. Evaluate investment alternatives using multiple decision attributes that include both financial and nonfinancial criteria.

4. Assess risk in evaluating investment alternatives.

5. Establish a management system that provides the cost and performance data needed to evaluate investment decisions.

The strategic plan is the starting point for the investment management decision process, and planning is a prerequisite to the execution and control of an investment. Sound investment management decisions therefore must tie directly to the long-term strategic plans and to the short-term goals of the company.

Performance measurement systems also should relate directly to company strategy. Measurements influence how people behave.

Changes in investment management decisions, such as those related to technology investments, are driven by company strategies and the firm's critical success factors. A firm's strategy for dealing with technological change influences how the firm invests in advanced manufacturing technology. Does the company want to be at the leading edge of technological change, or will the firm invest only in proven technology? This strategic decision influences the type and timing of the technology investments the company makes. Individual types of technology investments change with the specifics of product development plans and production forecasts.

Principle 2. Evaluate the investment alternatives consistently.

Use a reliable methodology to translate strategic objectives into measurable performance targets. The targets may be financial, nonfinancial, or a combination. For example, a company's strategy may require a new product to meet predefined safety and performance standards, as well as a specified return on investment.

The investment management process needs to be consistent with the firm's complexity levels to be sure that the firm meets strategic goals. The investment management process also should recognize that most major investments are interrelated elements of an integrated strategy. They are not independent projects.

The benefits of advanced technology investments are often synergistic—the linked benefits are larger than the separate benefits. A single robot provides some benefits, but the value of automation may increase geometrically when an entire CAD/CAM production line is in use. The synergistic nature of benefits (and costs or risks) requires a broad approach to investment analysis.

Principle 3. Evaluate investment alternatives using multiple decision attributes that include both financial and nonfinancial criteria.

Analysis of the costs and benefits associated with investment decisions requires a system. This system includes qualitative and quantitative criteria of a financial and nonfinancial nature.

Traditional financial measures, such as cash cost or return on investment, focus on a single aspect of the investment decision process. Improvements in quality, production flexibility, and employee motivation are of strategic importance. They represent a key part of cost/benefit analysis.

For example, when a new production process is evaluated, traditionally the cost of the equipment, labor, and material is taken into account. The cost savings that are associated with having fewer customer returns because of high product quality typically are not measured.

Quantification of such traditionally qualitative factors may be possible. Such quantification would permit the use of multiple attributes in the basic decision model. The analysis should be sufficiently comprehensive so that it captures all the critical decision factors.

Principle 4. Assess risk in evaluating investment alternatives.

Risk is inherent in investment decisions. Consider risk explicitly. Include uncertainties related to economic, commercial, technological, and implementation risks. An investment in advanced technology has each of these risk elements.

Installation may be more costly than was expected, which raises the economic cost. You may not realize all the expected revenues from the new equipment. A competitive product may offer similar features at a better price. Technological change may make the new equipment obsolete sooner than expected. Gaining full advantage of the equipment's features may be delayed. You may need to train employees and learn to adopt new operating procedures.

Principle 5. Establish a management system that provides the cost and performance data needed to evaluate investment decisions.

The management system should provide the data needed to monitor the investment individually and strategically. A company makes an advanced technology investment to achieve certain cost savings and quality improvements. The management system should permit the company to measure whether these cost savings and quality improvements occur.

The system also should allow review of unexpected costs or benefits that result from the investment decision. Usually an analysis of the success or failure of an investment management decision occurs only after the investment is made. Design the process to increase the potential for making successful investments because there is always investment risk. One purpose of the performance measurement system is to help guide future investment decisions.

The Investment Management Matrix

The investment management matrix, shown in Exhibit 1-2 and at the end of the book, is a tool that will help you determine the status of your company's investment management system. The matrix provides a framework for improving the investment management process. It has nine investment management steps grouped into four core processes. Both the core processes and the steps are on the horizontal axis. The vertical axis consists of five levels of business or investment complexity. The matrix cells list some of the processes, tools, and technologies associated with investment activity at that level of complexity.

The sequence of the core processes and steps in the matrix is logical for effective investment management.

Exhibit 1-2. THE INVESTMENT MANAGEMENT MATRIX

		Strategic Planning	Option Development	Decision Making	Execution and Tracking
	CORE PROCESSES: STEPS IN INVESTMENT MANAGEMENT PROCESS				
Levels of Complexity		1. Identify goals and objectives. 2. Establish performance targets.	3. Identify costs and cost drivers. 4. Identify alternative approaches.	5. Assess & analyze risks. 6. Evaluate investments. 7. Select an investment portfolio.	8. Integrate with cost management system. 9. Establish performance tracking system.
Level One		Bottom up list Top down mandates	Single key discipline defines	Based on available (budget) & "seat-of-the-pants" Investment in budget (blind faith)	Standard public data
Level Two		Capital strategy	Multidiscipline input	In-depth reviews Checklists Additional approval layers Standard approval forms	Progress reports Performance measures Audits
Level Three		Strategic choices	Based on cost management system data	Decision and risk analysis Decision models Customized presentations	Activity analysis & measures Life-cycle records
Level Four		Link/translation of strategy into performance measures, targets, goals, and objectives	Based on strategy	Decision-support systems Link proposals to strategy Performance-measure value	Performance management Continuous feedback
Level Five		Integral part of the cost management system—continuous improvement			

Strategic planning comes before option development, which precedes decision making. To be effective, the core process steps should be in balance at the proper level of complexity.

The core processes are consistent with traditional capital investment decision models but are significantly broader. For example, one approach to the capital investment decision process involves six distinct steps: collecting ideas, developing alternatives, estimating results, evaluating alternatives, considering risk, and post-auditing.

These steps fall primarily within the core processes of option development, decision making, and execution and tracking. No specific item on this list relates to strategic planning.

Use the Right Tools

Different levels of product, process, market, location, and operating complexity require distinct investment management tools. A firm may be simultaneously at several levels of complexity. The complexity of an investment decision also may change which investment management tools a firm should use.

The levels within each of the core processes are evolutionary and additive. As a company moves down the matrix for a particular type of complexity, it needs different skills, knowledge, and tools. It should add the information derived from the new processes to existing skills and tools.

A belief that you need an investment may be enough when you are directly responsible for an entire business. As the firm grows and others assume responsibility, you may support your belief by using checklists or standard approval steps.

*Later in the growth sequence, or when the invest-
ment decision is particularly important, you may
supplement these informal tools with detailed,
analytical reviews. Beliefs remain a key part of
the investment measurement process, however.*

The columns are connected. You should focus on
being at the same level across the core processes. If there
is not a balanced linkage across the investment management steps, you waste resources because you don't use
the tools effectively or because risks increase.

The output of the strategic planning process is input
to the option development process. You must understand
the nature of the input. Then you can select the proper
option development tools.

For instance, sometimes it is not cost effective to
have employees develop a variety of methods for making
a new product. This effort is wasted if the company
owner has no interest in adding a new product or
already knows the manufacturing process.

A change is necessary when the complexity level of
the company or the decision does not match the existing
tools and processes. For example, if one person makes all
the capital decisions in a multiple location company
without input from others, there is a complexity mis-
match.

When appropriate balance does not exist, system
changes will make investment decision making more
effective. You can improve the effectiveness of the
decision process by adding new tools.

Mindset for Improvement

When you determine there is an opportunity to
improve the investment management process, make
changes. Success requires a commitment to change by

top management and the persons responsible for the process. Certain requirements are necessary for change to occur. They are:

- Understand the guiding principles or assumptions.

- Know the steps in the investment management process and understand how they relate to the company's investment management practices.

- Identify the complexity level(s) of the company. Movement through the matrix steps occurs until the firm reaches the desired position in the investment management process.

- Identify the barriers to investment management improvement, then create and use a process to reduce the effect of these barriers.

There are several common barriers to successful investment management. For example, movement through the matrix modules often requires a cultural change. Business and investment strategies should be integrated with operating strategy, product flow, and product development.

The "Seven Cs" Model

Many change models could help resolve the problems of putting the CMS system in place. We briefly describe one, the seven Cs model (see Exhibit 1-3), as an aid in improvement planning.[1]

---

[1]From Michael D. Shields and S. Mark Young, *Implementing Cost Management Systems in Advanced Manufacturing Technology Firms: Behavioral and Organizational Strategies*, CAM-I, 1988.

Exhibit 1-3. THE SEVEN Cs MODEL

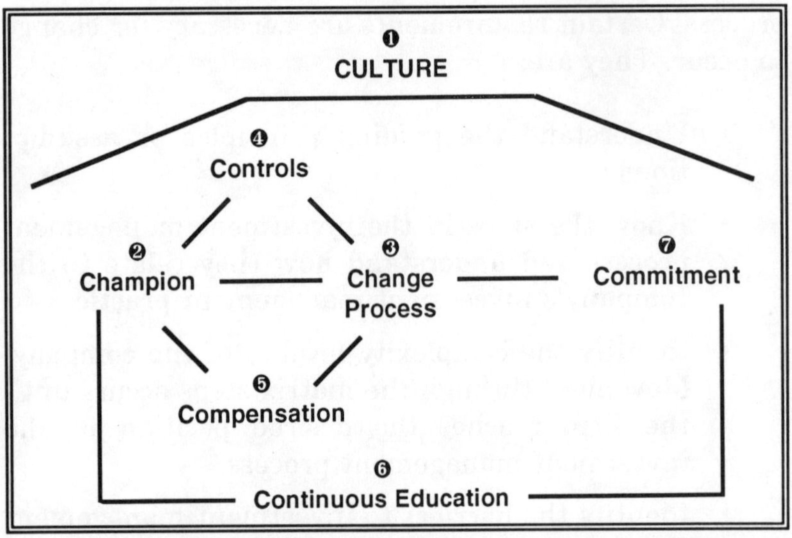

```
                              ❶
                           CULTURE

                       ❹
                     Controls

         ❷                        ❸                        ❼
     Champion ————————— Change ————————— Commitment
                                 Process

                       ❺
                  Compensation

                              ❻
                   Continuous Education
```

The model suggests that firms must move away from managing by traditional cost accounting measurements. A company needs broader concepts of management and should focus on process, not on product or function. This focus requires both structural and behavioral changes in the organization. A model such as the seven Cs can help make the change process work.

Culture, the first C, is "the way we do things around here." An organizational culture can be strongly functional, or it can be dysfunctional, or weak. The remaining six Cs combine to support a change in culture. The change strategy must match the situation in the organization.

Identify a *champion* for investment management, the second C. The champion must be a capable change agent, positioned at the appropriate organizational level.

- The investment management champion works to develop processes that permit project champions to function effectively and efficiently.

- A multifunctional implementation team should address issues such as the effects of a system on short-term profit, what performance measures make the system work, and the need for changes in work-force skills.

The champion would lead the investment management implementation team in planning the *change process,* the third C.

- Different situations require diverse change strategies.

- Successful implementation typically requires evolutionary change strategies.

- A coordinated top down and bottom up approach eases the change process. Clear, consistent management direction, combined with input and personnel education, are critical to a successful change plan.

Controls, the fourth C, increase the rate of continuous improvement and the chance of achieving a firm's strategy. When the company has chosen and used its controls carefully, the success of the implementation is more likely.

Develop *compensation* approaches that reward team performance, skills of individual members, the long term; and risk taking. Compensation, the fifth C, should support an investment management process focused on continuous improvement.

Continuous education, the sixth C, is an essential support factor for cultural changes and helps generate innovative ideas.

Finally, you need *commitment*, the seventh C, throughout the organization to support each of the Cs.

The congruence of controls, compensation, and continuous education support the change process. They help you get the needed commitment.

Summary

Identifying and evaluating investment opportunities are an important part of the management system. Opportunities for improving the investment management process exist. You should understand the guiding principles, the core process steps, the level of investment and organizational complexity, and the tools and technologies.

Effective investment management can take many forms. We identified five guiding principles important for an effective process and introduced the investment management matrix, a tool that helps a company clarify the status of its investment management system. The matrix provides the framework for improving the investment management process. Finally, we suggested a change model to help you overcome the barriers to changing investment procedures.

Chapter 2

Core Process Steps

Investment management has four core processes. Exhibit 2-1 lists the nine steps included in the four core processes. (The entire investment management matrix is shown at the end of the book.) We briefly explain each core process in this chapter. Later chapters discuss the individual process steps in more detail.

Exhibit 2-1. CORE PROCESSES AND STEPS

Core Processes	Steps
A. Strategic Planning	1. Identify goals and objectives. 2. Establish performance measures and targets.
B. Option Development	3. Identify costs and cost drivers. 4. Identify alternative approaches.
C. Decision Analysis	5. Assess and analyze risks. 6. Evaluate investments. 7. Select an investment portfolio.
D. Execution and Tracking	8. Integrate investment management into the cost management system. 9. Establish performance tracking system.

Strategic Planning

Strategic planning defines the objectives of and constraints on a company's operations. This process is
integral to identifying the organization's goals. It is critical to set performance measures and targets. Information comes from the corporate mission, from competitive
strategies, and from an awareness of financial constraints.

The strategic planning core process has two steps.
You take these steps to derive information from the
strategic plan and then use the information in the
investment process.

Step 1. Identify goals and objectives.

Specifying organizational goals and objectives is part
of the strategic planning process. Senior management
agrees upon, prioritizes, and communicates these goals
to the entire company.

The first step of the investment management process
involves translating these corporate strategies, such as
revenue growth, market share, and profitability, into
specific and measurable divisional, product, and operating goals.

The goals for different segments of the organization
should be consistent with the overall corporate strategies. An understanding of these goals should help
individuals set priorities for projects.

For example, forecasts of product demand and machine performance requirements directly influence the
investments made in production equipment. This goal
identification is critical for effective investment management. The expression of consistent goals and objectives
varies by organizational level. Exhibit 2-2 shows these
differences.

Exhibit 2-2. VARYING GOALS

Level	Goal
Corporate	• Earn a 12% return on equity. • Earn the Baldrige award.
Division X	• Make a profit of $4.5 million. • Provide 18% return on assets. • Improve customer satisfaction to 99.5%.
Product Y	• Generate $900,000 in sales. • Make an operating profit of 14%. • Meet on-time delivery targets every time.
Operation A	• Deliver part A for $.20 each. • Provide part A within 30 minutes of order.

Step 2. Establish performance measures and targets.

You need performance measures and targets consistent with the goals of the firm. Different perspectives for measuring company activities mean several types of performance measurements are used.

- The stockholders or investors have a financial perspective for measuring results.

- Customers (internal and external) measure results against their needs.

- Business functions measure processes using their functional orientation.

- The firm measures innovation and improvements on an incremental and on a total basis.

These differences make distinct types of measurements part of this step.

- Financial performance measures are specified, such as the net present value of investment cash flows and the return on investment.

- Nonfinancial quantitative performance measures are created—process yield, schedule attainment, and customer problems resolved.

- Qualitative performance measures are designed, such as product obsolescence and customer satisfaction.

Which measurements are appropriate? The answer differs with the level and functional area of the organization. The criteria used for selecting all measures should be consistent with the shared goals of the firm. Different types of measures are combined to make performance consistent with the company's objectives.

Analysis of a proposed machine may suggest that it has an expected cost of $5 million. The net present value is $3 million, the expected yield is 98%, and customer satisfaction should improve recognizably. A relative weight for each of these measures could be part of a performance measurement model. For instance, you could assign a relative weight of 5% to the expected cost while giving 30% to achieving a 98% yield.

Practically, the complexity level of a company will affect the types of measurements used. As the investment management process evolves, qualitative measures could become nonfinancial quantitative measures. They also may become a more important part of the decision process.

> *A company may find it desirable to develop procedures to assign cash flow savings to improvements in product quality. These savings include the reduction in rework and the reduction in product returns and warranty claims that result from better quality. A qualitative measure—quality—may tie directly to a financial evaluation process such as net present value.*

Option Development

Investment opportunities relate to many aspects of an organization's activities. For instance, you may make capital investments for replacement, expansion of existing operations, expansion into new activities, advanced technology, administrative improvement, or social need. The option development process helps identify and classify the factors that distinguish investment opportunities.

Option development focuses on generating investment alternatives using the differences between the "as is" and the "to be" business environment. The gap between what should be and what is represents an opportunity. The strategic plan provides a starting point for opportunity identification. Then the option development process helps formulate alternatives that will respond to investment opportunities and achieve long-range goals.

Step 3. Identify costs and cost drivers.

The purpose of this step is to identify the costs and cost drivers associated with an existing or planned product or process. Improved accuracy in the measurement of costs, such as that achieved with activity-based systems, enhances investment decision making. This step provides more reliable data for the evaluation process.

Once the costs and cost drivers (causes of cost) have been identified, you can examine investment opportunities designed to change the cost structure.

- Many investments are made specifically to reduce cost. Analysis of an investment decision requires knowledge of existing and potential costs and an understanding of what factors actually drive these costs. Cost management information has new dimensions, such as activity accounting, value-added analysis, and target costing. Each may be important for this step of the investment management process.

- Investments focused on reducing the causes of costs and nonvalue-added costs are part of the investment process. You need to prioritize them to meet the firm's goals.

- You may need certain investments to achieve cost or performance results consistent with management-defined targets.

The increased analytical capability provided by modern cost management systems permits individuals and teams to quantify important competitive factors. Activity-based accounting helps link quantitative financial and quantitative nonfinancial factors. These nonfinancial elements play an important role in investment decisions. Activities also become the common denominator for evaluation purposes. For example, you can analyze excess capacity, bottlenecks, or lost potential using activity analysis.

A newspaper publisher deferred acquisition of an additional press by investing in more efficient word processing software. With this software, final copy could be prepared 30 minutes faster than before, effectively extending the press deadline. The added time allowed the firm to run current presses longer. The activity of word processing was the key. Conventional investment justification methodologies would not have shown an acceptable payback on the software as a stand-alone project. Without option analysis the publisher might not have made the word processing investment, particularly in a capital-scarce environment. Instead, the firm would have saved the capital to buy the additional printing press.

Identifying costs and cost drivers by means of techniques such as activity-based costing forces the company to use multidiscipline inputs. Increasingly these efforts are relating to the other management data or to explicit strategy perspectives.

Textronix circuit board manufacturing operations set a strategic goal of achieving the industry's highest return on investment. Using activity-based cost analysis, the firm identified and changed costs and cost drivers with the help of a CIM (computer-integrated manufacturing) system. One result was the decision to abandon certain types of products because they were inconsistent with the capital investment in technology in a particular factory. Concentrating on products compatible with the plant capital structure helped the plant meet the strategic goal.[1]

---

[1]Presentation by Gene Hendrickson and Terri Volpe of Textronix at June 1991 CAM-I meeting.

We don't discuss the extensive body of literature on cost and cost driver identification in this guide. However, the work in the activity-based management area is an important part of the management process. The results of this work already are influencing the tools and processes identified in several cells of the investment management matrix.

Step 4. Identify alternative approaches.

You should identify investment opportunities and generate alternatives for each opportunity, using appropriate option development techniques. The goal is to show that you examined alternatives for the existing opportunity.

- You should consider ideas generated by various parts of the organization.

- The extent of the search for alternatives should be in proportion to the importance of the investment opportunity and the structure of the problem. You will find that some opportunities are well structured, others are semistructured, and some are essentially unstructured.

Option development is considered in more detail in Chapter 4.

Decision Making

Decision analysis and decision making often are emphasized most in the investment management process. Much has been written about analytical techniques, risk evaluation methods, and other aspects of the decision process. It is only one of the four investment management core processes, however.

Step 5. Assess and analyze risks.

An investment decision typically involves economic, commercial, technological, and implementation risks. Each risk type requires you to consider distinctive factors during project analysis.

- When there is *economic* or *commercial risk,* an investment for many reasons may not produce the projected benefits. Examples include changes in government regulations, inflation rate changes, interest rate movement, competition from other entities, and time and resource constraints.

- With *technological risk* the investment may fail to achieve the expected manufacturing or service benefits. Higher risks are associated with leading edge applications. For critical systems management issues you may need to develop a contingency plan. Technological risk factors include hardware failure, software failure, lack of vendor support, contingency requirements, and communication failures.

- *Implementation risk* is the failure to achieve desired levels of knowledge, skills, and attributes. These risks are numerous and include those related to employee attitudes and skills, personnel education and training, and the learning curve of the technical support staff. Employee reward systems and customer acceptance are also part of implementation risk.

Risk management plans include procedures to reduce risks and increase benefits. You develop plans after identifying the significant risk factors that may influence the project outcome. The plans should reflect potential risks and contingencies and should track any expected benefits.

Using a variety of tools and processes to analyze the risks associated with an investment decision will help the firm moderate the effects of each type of risk. We discuss several of the tools for this analysis later in this guide.

Step 6. Evaluate investments.

To evaluate investment alternatives, you need to consider qualitative and quantitative costs and benefits. Conventional investment methods, such as payback and net present value (NPV), focus on the cash flows associated with a single potential investment.

These conventional methods for the most part are concerned with marginal issues. For example, when is net present value better than internal rate of return (IRR)? Now more attention is given to the basic uncertainties associated with cash flow estimates and to the limitations of using only cash flows for investment analysis.

Cash flow analysis, cycle time, and flexibility are critical to the investment analysis process. Approaches that are designed specifically to consider other factors may be important, particularly for complex organizations. Examples of such approaches include the uncertainties of individual project cash flows, the interrelationships among investment alternatives, and qualitative factors.

Multiple attribute scoring models, portfolio analysis models, and decision support systems may help in comparing investment alternatives. These tools are considered in more detail in Chapter 5.

Step 7. Select an investment portfolio.

Investment analysis and evaluation is one tool that leads to a decision on a single project or a group of related investments. Processes and procedures set up in the risk analysis and evaluation steps should result in selection decisions consistent with company goals. New evaluation technologies may provide complex companies with better information than the single-project tools now in common use.

Execution and Tracking

Once you make investment decisions, you must have an implementation plan. Which employees and parts of the organization are responsible for acquisition, construction, testing, and integration of the investment into the firm? You usually know who has these responsibilities for basic investment decisions. As the investment decision process becomes more complex, suitable organizational structures must be in place for executing investment decisions efficiently and effectively.

For example, project execution is important for an investment in advanced technology equipment. The execution requires coordinating the purchase, setup, and testing of the equipment with programs to educate and train employees. Otherwise, the benefits of the new technology may not develop.

Step 8. Integrate investment management into the cost management system.

The investment management process is one essential part of the total management system. Other elements include budgeting, performance measurement, internal control, and special project analysis. Making certain that these segments work together in a coordinated fashion is very important. Studies of the capital budgeting practices used by large companies often have shown a weak or nonexistent linkage between the investment analysis process and performance evaluation.

Integration of the investment management system into the total management system helps a firm reach goals. It increases the benefits of the cost management system.

Step 9. Establish a performance tracking system.

Periodic or continuous evaluation of investment decisions is part of traditional capital investment—sometimes it is called the post-audit. Post-audits often are single-point events rather than continuous evaluations, but this step suggests a need to track investment performance. Below are examples of parts of a performance tracking system (we explore them later in the book).

- *An activity-based accounting system* tracks the activities affecting the criteria that were the basis for the initial investment decision. An activity approach provides a clearer picture of the incremental effects of activities than a conventional (functional or product) reporting system does.

- *Technology accounting* helps you evaluate the asset in a cause-and-effect relationship.

- *Target costing* compares actual costs with the benchmark performance of an investment over its life cycle. The process is useful when there are variances from plan and to exploit further opportunities and manage risk.

In practical terms the execution and tracking step cuts across much of the investment management process. An ideal cost benefit tracking system includes the following steps:

1. Identify the critical data elements and the cost and performance measures for the investment.
2. Assess the existing cost benefit data on individual investments and portfolios of investments.
3. Develop a usable methodology to validate cost benefit data.
4. Design a conceptual cost benefit tracking system for different types of investments.
5. Test investment models by comparing actual results with cost baselines; then analyze the differences.
6. Develop procedures for responding to differences that arise.
7. Design a cost benefit reporting system.
8. Install the system.
9. Use feedback from the system to evaluate investment performance.

An example of the project tracking used by one firm is the project benefits matrix described below.

The firm divided measures of the project's benefits into areas of functionality, cost, schedule, and quality. As the project moved through its milestones, the benefit claims—factors such as material savings, employee reduction, and process cycle time reduction—were quantified. This tracking permitted monitoring of benefit claims at each milestone. The firm also monitored claims in one-year and three-year post-audits.

This type of process helps a firm emphasize good project management practices, use a balanced process, and learn from past decisions.

Summary

The four core processes and nine steps represent one piece of the investment management process. They should be part of the process in your firm. The changes needed in your existing decision process depend on the assessments you make of your company's capabilities and on your decisions about required or desirable improvements. These decisions require a recognition of the complexity levels of the organization and the investment. You also must be aware of the variety of investment management tools and technologies available. The following chapters describe and illustrate the influence of complexity on the investment management process and the tools and technologies to handle it.

Chapter 3

The Core Processes and Complexity Levels

The investment management process evolves as the firm or the decision grows progressively more complex. A company needs to improve its decision procedures as it moves down through the various complexity levels identified in the investment management matrix (see page 116).

Each intersection of a level of complexity with a process is a cell. The proper approaches, techniques, and tools differ for each cell in the investment management process.

Dealing with Complexity

In analyzing the complexity of the investment decisions that a firm must make, an issue is how to assess decision complexity. Is it based on the number of factors important for the decision or is it the interrelationship of these factors? Maybe the risks and rewards associated with making a better or worse decision should be assessed.

When dealing with investment decision complexity it is important to discover the answers to several questions.

- Where is the investment decision made? Where did the information that was used to make the decision originate?

- What kind of information is needed to decide on an investment? What methods are used to gather and interpret that information?

- What types of options are being considered?

In each case, complexity correlates directly with the organizational structure needed for a sound investment decision. A decision to replace one automobile in a fleet involves less complexity than the decision to build a new plant or introduce a product. Different tools and techniques are appropriate. Complex decisions require more complex tools.

The Levels of Complexity

The levels in the matrix also relate directly to the complexity of the organization. The more complex the firm, the higher the level of investment management tools and procedures necessary for the process. Structural complexity of the company is a key indicator of which process should be in place. Remember, factors related to the decision itself also may change the level. There are five structural levels of complexity.

Level One: Very Simple

This complexity level is typical of owner/manager firms or entrepreneurial business operations. The decision maker is involved directly in all aspects of the day-to-day management. The individual has personal knowledge of all operations, issues, and other factors that affect the company. Decision making is rapid and informal.

Level Two: Simple

This level of complexity is typical of partnerships. The "decision maker" is actually a small group of people or a management team directly involved in all aspects of the business. The people who make the decisions collectively know at first hand all operations, issues, and other factors that affect the firm.

In an alternative form, the top manager uses reports from knowledgeable individuals to make the investment decisions. Communication combines all the collective knowledge of these persons into a comprehensive process of investment management.

Level Three: Basic

At this level, the top decision maker (chief executive) does not have personal knowledge of all functions or areas. The firm consists of business units organized by function or discipline, business type, or geographical location. Each unit has a manager directly involved in all aspects of the day-to-day management of that unit. Each leader personally knows his or her area's operations, issues, and other factors.

Unit managers make the initial decisions. They then come together to advise the chief executive (top manager). At these decision meetings the key people share data and resolve issues between the units they lead. The communication process and tools become more formal to promote consistency and allow for comparisons that improve the investment decisions.

Level Four: Complex

Complexity exists because there are several layers of management, based on a functional organization. The company may be organized by discipline, by region, or by business type. Multifunction teams review information and prepare recommendations for the decision makers. Networks allow the decision makers to share and discuss the data, even if they are not physically in the same place.

Investment management tools and procedures must be more formal for this type of company. This complex structure is typical of most large public companies. It allows firms to operate multinationally and as conglomerates.

Level Five: Very Complex

At this level, various parts of the organization may differ. Some parts may be broken down by region, others by discipline, and still others by business. Explicitly defined organizational reporting lines may not even exist. This firm either: (1) operates on a global basis, (2) has many diverse types of businesses, or (3) both. Decision making in such a firm requires dealing with fragmented data and making trade-offs among competing business unit recommendations for using the firm's limited resources.

The decision-making process requires sharing data with many people, who are at different places at different times. Coordinating the operations of the firm and decision making requires alliances, partnerships, trust, delegation, and a mechanism for strategic deployment. This very complex form is the global business model that is the goal of many very large firms.

Not having the right systems in place to manage the firm's investments properly becomes a barrier to success. To move from a level four (multinational) operation to a level five (global) company requires more than a change in the organization chart. The firm must improve its systems and manage more complex investment decisions effectively.

Types of Investment Decisions

There are many types of investment decisions. Each class of decision may occur at a different level of complexity. Some firms make very complex decisions having to do with research and development or marketing investment. Meanwhile, their decisions about investments in manufacturing facilities are straightforward and simple.

Other firms may make their most complex investment decisions in the areas of training or new technology investments. The tools and techniques that a firm uses should be consistent with the complexity of the decisions. Therefore, different levels in the matrix may be appropriate for different decisions made by the same company.

A complex (level four) organization permits managers to make smaller, capital equipment decisions, within the constraints of a budget. There is no extensive review or analysis by other levels of the company. This level four company in terms of organizational complexity requires only tools and procedures from level one or level two for this type of decision. The unit manager's knowledge of the business is adequate.

More specific illustrations of how investment complexity differs from organizational complexity are part of the later discussion of core process steps.

The matrix is useful in assessing the current methods, approaches, and systems for managing investments. The methodology for each step in the investment management process should be appropriate for the level of complexity of the investment decisions or for the complexity of the firm itself.

- Approaches designed for less complex situations than those that exist carry a significant risk of not dealing effectively and comprehensively with the problems. These situations result in inappropriate decisions or faulty execution of the right decision.

- Approaches that are too complex for the situation waste valuable resources.

- Unbalanced approaches, those where some methods are appropriate for more complex situations, are wasteful and ineffective.

You can improve the investment management process if the current approach for a particular type of investment is not appropriate for the decision complexity level. Take care when making changes, however. The change process should be an evolutionary journey, not a revolutionary one. Move up or down one row at a time. Try to keep the entire row in balance as you make changes.

The first changes you make should be those needed to get the row in balance. Then you can change the level of the entire process. If your firm must use more complex tools than the existing system can handle, external consultants may help bridge the gap while the firm develops its own internal capabilities.

Guard against creating "superb silos." In other words, don't operate at a high level for one step of the process while leaving the other areas at a lower level. This imbalance wastes resources and destroys the linkage between the process steps.

For example, assume the organization develops very complex systems for option selection but retains primitive ones for strategic planning. As a result, the firm will micro-manage decisions—a wasteful process. In addition, investment decisions will not relate properly to the real strategies of the company.

The investment management process is more successful when the core processes are linked. For example, the output of the strategic planning process is the input to the option development process. If a company does not move to level four of the strategic planning process before moving to level four of option development, problems and inconsistencies are likely to develop.

The five levels of complexity often cause an evolutionary journey of investment management implementation. A company that is moving down the matrix within any of the core process steps continually adds new skills, knowledge, and tools. Even so, progression to the next level becomes necessary only when there is a need to improve the existing decision data.

Evolution Through the Core Processes

Evolution Through the Strategic Planning Process

The strategic planning process includes two investment management steps: (1) identify goals and objectives and (2) establish performance targets.

At the first level of complexity two strategic planning techniques are common. One is developing "bottom up" lists. The second is using budgets while top management mandates investment goals and performance targets. These mandates include plans to do what the law requires and plans for which no options exist.

Problems in the strategic planning process move a firm to the second complexity level. The typical approach is to use a capital strategy process that emphasizes cash and total expenditure budgets for capital projects.

A company reaches the third level of strategic planning when it recognizes that it cannot achieve all its

identified strategic goals and objectives. It then develops
a strategic choice model to select the proper strategies.
Concurrently, it supplements short-term financial
measures with reviews of the life cycle of each investment opportunity. In addition, firms often introduce the
effects of the goals and plans on shareholder value (or
values associated with other stakeholders).

At the fourth level, a firm views most potential
investments as an interrelated part of a few portfolios of
investments. At this level, a company can deal with
disinvestment or abandonment strategies, which are part
of the normal strategic planning process. They are
normal as opposed to being considered a crisis or disrup-
tion in the process. The competencies developed permit
the firm to incorporate into the strategy both target
costing and process costing of products or services.

Finally, in the fifth stage, all the discrete methods
and technologies of strategic planning have been mas-
tered. The firm reviews and renews its strategy continuously. It applies those pieces that fit the current situation and needs.

Evolution Through the Option Development Process

Option development includes the step that identifies
alternate approaches and the step used to define cost
and identify the causes of cost.

At level one of option development, a single discipline defines the available investment alternatives. In
some firms this discipline might be marketing, in others,
engineering or perhaps research and development.

At level two problems or performance shortfalls are
identified, and other disciplines begin to provide investment option input. An interactive process provides
management with better identification of alternatives,

and management develops a more definitive understanding of what drives investment costs and creates investment benefits.

The third stage introduces advanced cost management systems methods into the investment process. Activity analysis and technology accounting are among the techniques used to identify and define opportunities.

The fourth level brings a major addition to the option development core processes—scenario development. At this level the investment process involves all appropriate disciplines, the identification of all costs and their drivers, and an understanding of existing interdependencies. The investment team defines and considers mutually exclusive scenarios.

Again, the final level is mastery of the process for developing options and scenarios. Review and renewal are critical to the retention of mastery.

Evolution Through the Decision Making Process

The third core process, decision analysis, includes three process steps: (1) assess and analyze risks, (2) evaluate investments, and (3) select an investment portfolio.

At the first level, investment decisions are experience-based "seat-of-the-pants" judgments. Questions such as, "Are there dollars available in the budget?" often define decisions. Unless the decision maker is careful, political or "first pig to the trough" approaches for funding investments can be the result. In this initial stage, investment proposals are part of the budget. People often assume that the budget represents the enterprise's strategy and will yield the desired financial results. As progression through the levels occurs, judgment remains part of the process, even as the firm introduces other technology and techniques.

At the second level, the rigor of the management review has increased, introducing in-depth scrutiny, checklists, and additional approvals. Second-stage investment proposals are aligned with approved capital strategies. Multidepartment or multifunction input and approval forms aid in analysis. Participants add new criteria and approvals to avoid repeating past mistakes. Thus, intangible factors start to appear, and the firm begins to address political or interpersonal issues.

The third level introduces risk and decision models into the process. Most of them focus on a single criterion such as return on investment (ROI), net present value (NPV), or schedule attainment. Firms also might use techniques such as the multiple attribute decision models (MADM) discussed in Chapter 5. Third-stage proposals need to be consistent with an enterprise's strategic choices. The decision and risk analysis processes furnish insight into key issues, and risk also is considered at this level.

At the fourth level, investment decision technology moves from using discrete models to using decision support systems (DSS). The process explicitly considers interrelationships and dependencies. Proposal preparations are consistent with the firm's strategies and emphasize the investment's effects on performance measures. Participants build consensus and commitment as a proposal moves to the decision point. An extended investment proposal shows the impact on customer needs, core corporate competencies, and key performance measures.

When a firm reaches level five of decision making, investment analysis may use an artificial intelligence-based expert system. Project champions might even use decision support systems (models) to test alternatives. The process demonstrates the impact of decision criteria. To encourage continuous improvement, investment decisions influence the reward system. New or altered performance measures are linked to rewards.

Evolution Through the Execution and Tracking Process

The final core process, execution and tracking, includes the step designed to integrate investment management with the total management system and the step that establishes a tracking system to obtain essential data for project control and strategic planning.

At level one, there is no formal tie between the investment management decision process and the overall management system. Investment tracking, if done, is selective. The focus is on what tax and regulatory agencies require or on the information needed to close the books.

By the second stage, there are additional audits closely aligned with decision analysis reviews. A firm begins to create and use formal progress reports, to develop performance measures, and to set up post-investment review procedures. Concurrently, tracking provides feedback against specific performance measures.

Integration of the investment management system with the overall management system requires management support. This support starts at the second level when management identifies the need for integration and tracking. It continues through the remaining stages of evolution.

In the third stage, members of the organization must be trained to use new approaches, tools, and techniques. For instance, performance data measurements are related to the life cycle of a decision or investment, providing input for strategic planning. The firm may introduce activity accounting, a technique that uses a collection of financial and nonfinancial performance information associated with significant activities of the firm. The technique helps identify and measure nonvalue-adding costs. It encourages valuation and quantification of factors such as quality, flexibility, and cycle times. People must be trained to use these techniques.

As a company moves toward the fourth level, it continues to introduce new technology and approaches for integrating the execution and tracking steps into the system. At this point the company is developing performance management techniques and continuous feedback systems that require the skill-building expertise of internal consultants or analysts.

In the fourth stage, tracking multiple attribute performance data should tie to the performance management processes. Based on the principle that consequences drive behavior, the measurement and tracking system drives the correct behavior identified in the investment management process. A company can reinforce and accelerate positive results and can address and correct negative results. Thus, investment management can align behavior management with strategic goals through the tracking system.

The fourth level also introduces sophisticated post-audits. They improve the quality of future investment decisions, provide a means for correction, or help a firm to make abandonment decisions. This type of post-audit is not a single event. It is a continuing process that occurs throughout the project life cycle. The most basic objective of the review and evaluation process is to identify potential errors or biases in making appraisals of proposed capital investments, so that the process can be improved.

Finally, total integration with the cost management system (CMS) occurs in stage five. This stage also brings mastery of efficiency and effectiveness procedures within the tracking system. These procedures provide data to reinforce desirable behavior patterns.

Summary

The extent of progress through the evolutionary stages of the investment management process will vary. Progress depends on the perceived need to improve. This need, in turn, relates directly to the complexity of the investment decisions. To be fully effective, a firm must use the same level of complexity in each of the core processes. The core process steps must balance.

Factors such as size, product or service complexity, and level of competition also strongly influence where an entity finds itself on the matrix for each process step. The examples and discussions in the following chapters provide more descriptions of several aspects of the process. The key to an effective investment management system is balance—balance in the process steps at the right complexity level. These chapters will help you integrate the tools and techniques your firm uses with the investment management matrix.

Chapter 4

Strategic Planning and Option Development

The CMS investment management methodology includes nine steps within four core processes. The rest of this guide provides an expanded explanation of these process steps and examines selected tools and technologies used at various complexity levels. You don't need the most sophisticated tools to have an effective investment management process, but you must balance process steps and complexity levels.

This chapter focuses on the first two core processes, strategic planning and option development.[1] Descriptions and examples illustrate the linkage that should exist between the steps at each of the complexity levels.

The Strategic Planning Process

Strategic planning in any organization is a multidimensional process. A single individual, a small group, or a team of participants will use different implementation techniques.

---

[1]Material in this chapter draws heavily on a research study by Roderick J. Reasor and William J. Sullivan, *A Conceptual Framework of Option Development Process Tools for the CAM-I CMS Investment Management Guide*, CAM-I, December 1991.

The firm uses a wider variety of strategic tools as it progresses to more complex organizational or investment levels. A more diverse group of managers becomes active in the strategic planning process as the firm grows. The basic concepts and beliefs that guide the firm's choices and behavior influence organizational strategy. The firm translates the basic character and vision into the specific corporate strategies, which determine where the business will compete. The result shows broadly how resources will be used within the company.

Corporate strategies have the following purposes:

- They establish the goals, purposes, and objectives of the company.

- They produce the principal policies and plans used to achieve the goals.

- They define the range of the firm's business.

- They define the characteristics of the organization.

- Finally, they define the values that should result for shareholders, employees, customers, and communities.

Once the firm has decided on its corporate strategies, it can develop and use individual business or product strategies that affect how it competes. Strategy includes goals for factors such as growth, market share, and profitability. The firm identifies investment opportunities at this level and positions itself among competitors.

Complexity Level and Strategy

How a firm develops strategies at the corporate level, the business level, or the product level depends partially on its complexity level. Strategy may come from the entrepreneurial insight of a single individual. Conceptually this insight may occur at any level of complexity, but it is more likely at levels one or two. By level three, the basic organizational structure has become complex enough that the firm requires strategic input from business unit managers.

This complexity influences the total investment strategy even when entrepreneurial insight is the primary driver. The perceived investment needs of unit managers and their implicit strategic choices change the overall plan.

Strategy also may be the result of systematic planning and analysis. Beyond level one, the planning process requires companies to use teams of decision makers who are organized on a functional or cross-functional basis. These teams consider all aspects of the organization.

Managers with direct involvement in all parts of their business units, along with top management, develop a strategic plan, using structured methods for making strategic investment choices. In a level three organization the decision makers may share data and resolve problems by completing this planning and analysis in a group meeting.

As organizational complexity increases, several layers of management and varied discipline, region, or business types develop and use the strategic plan. Linkages between the strategy and performance measures, targets, and goals become more specific. The investment process is effective.

Mastery of the strategic planning core process requires a well-structured mechanism for developing and integrating strategies. You need a good fit between the levels of organizational and investment complexity. The approach typically evolves into a more formal process at higher complexity levels even if a single person guides the basic strategies.

Ideally, the strategy development process should be systematic. It is right for the company applying the process. Strategy sometimes develops ad hoc, however, because the organization reacts to current problems instead of taking a systematic approach.

This situation happens most often when balance is lacking between the complexity level of the organization and the investment. The firm then uses the wrong strategic planning tools to identify objectives or to set performance targets.

> *The inventor of Company X's primary product runs the firm and continues to be active in product development. The firm has grown large enough so that he is no longer an active part of the production or marketing effort of the firm. He does, however, continue to dictate company goals and performance measures, without getting advice from unit managers.*

> *When the firm was small, manufacturing enough product was the problem. This problem resulted in a strategy—the firm would never be capital constrained. A key performance measurement, customer orders not filled in three days, was the result.*

> *Now the firm has 40% more capacity than needed to meet product demand. It always can fill customer orders from inventory. The strategic process is unbalanced. What worked when the firm was at complexity level one no longer works, and resources are wasted. The firm now is at least a level three organization. Improvements in the investment process would result from suitable linkages.*

Exhibit 4-1. GROWTH-SHARE MATRIX

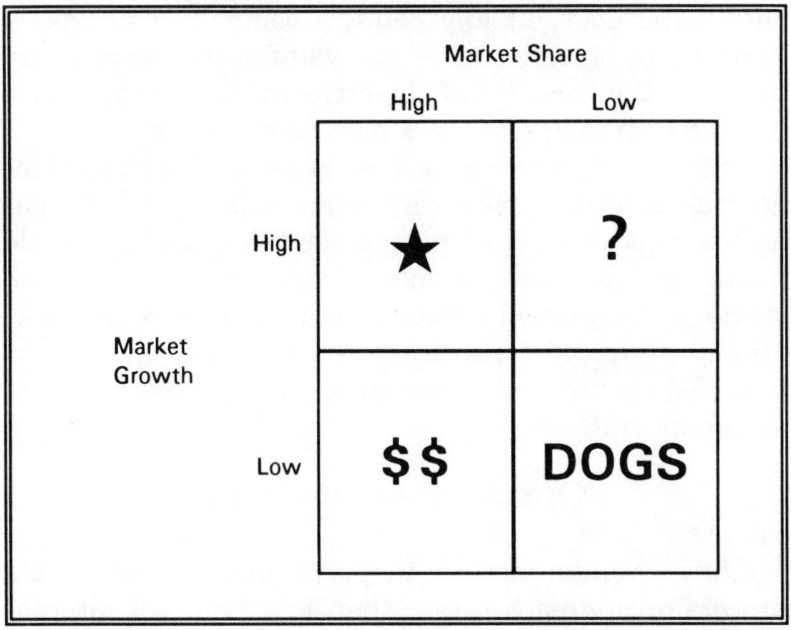

An Illustration

The growth-share matrix[2] illustrated in Exhibit 4-1 helps specify the types of investment opportunities that a company may identify through strategic planning.

Presumably most new investment opportunities will be for the stars. Both the market share and growth of the stars are high. There will be some investment for the question marks, which have high market growth but low current market share. You should keep the cash cows to

---

[2]Many variations of this matrix have been developed, written about, and used by various individuals and companies. This variation was abstracted from Reasor and Sullivan, op. cit. The original matrix is attributed to the Boston Consulting Group.

supply capital to other business units within the firm.
Divest the dogs. At any point, a company will have a
portfolio of investments. Some will fall into each group
because the results of investment are uncertain—
investments made for stars may be unsuccessful.

Strategic planning is important because it helps
identify opportunities for investment. You should focus
on the gaps that exist between what is and what should
be. In addition to the form(s) of strategic analysis used,
strategy formulation influences administrative consider-
ations. Financial constraints and the CEO's stated or
unstated agenda and approach to strategic management
are important.

Option Development

It is human nature to patch and repair an old
process or approach rather than focus on new alternatives. In making investment decisions, companies and
people often focus most on incremental changes in what
already is being done.

> *A company manufactures a product using a
> three-step process. Each step is a separate respon-
> sibility unit. Capital decisions often focus on
> what type of equipment can complete each step
> fastest. Decisions based on the lowest labor cost
> within the manufacturing cell are common. This
> company may not be directing enough attention
> to changes in the plant layout that could reduce
> inventory and lower other manufacturing costs.*

Option development techniques help you analyze
problems and generate new ideas. Option development
methods force you to focus attention on alternatives.
Knowledge of the costs and the cost drivers associated

with investments improves the decision-making process.

The problem statement flows from the strategic planning process to the option development process. Creative problem-solving techniques can help generate possible solutions. You may make an effort to examine the problem in a different way. You may redefine the problem. You may break the problem into its major parts and use each piece to identify possible solutions.

Assume that a $.02 piece of a $40 product frequently breaks. Initially we may assume the solution is to strengthen this part so it doesn't fail. Analysis of the techniques for improving the part may be costly. If we reformulate the problem, different solution options may surface. Let's state the problem as "find a way the customer can continue to use the tool if this part fails." The option of including a replacement part (costing $.02) and installation instructions (costing $.04) is suggested. This solution may keep the customer happy and be better for the firm. Even if the part breaks, the customer can quickly repair and use the product. The company also avoids the costs of processing a repair claim and sending a replacement part.

In the example, both option development steps are part of the suggested solution. The costs and cost drivers associated with the repair were identified. Then alternatives for dealing with the problem were generated.

There are a wide variety of option development techniques. They can be split into two general groups.

*   *Redefinitional techniques* seek to examine the problem in a different manner. They provide new perspectives on the problem.

- *Analytical techniques* help break the problem into its major elements. You then may identify possible interrelationships among these elements. It may be easier to focus on the variables critical for the investment.

You can use redefinitional and analytical techniques at any level of option development. These methods require only an initial problem statement. Once you identify the problem, you can redefine or analyze it into opportunities.

Creative problem solving requires idea generation. Techniques for generating ideas are the core of the option development process. New methods develop regularly, but we can classify the techniques in three ways:

- Individual and group techniques.

- Brainstorming and brainwriting methods. A small, interacting group generates ideas verbally in brainstorming. The group generates ideas silently in brainwriting.

- Free association and forced association techniques. Experiences or the immediate environment are used in the free association method. Ideas occur by chance. In forced relationship methods two or more elements are forced together to generate ideas. Practical ideas are more likely to come from related elements, however.

You can classify individual idea-generation techniques according to the problem scope. Problems may be broad, medium, or narrow. Group idea-generation techniques are classified by problem scope and complexity, by the importance of training people in technique usage, and by implementation difficulty.

Usually, you should:

- Select techniques similar in complexity to the problem.

- Select techniques proportional in implementation difficulty to the need to solve the problem.

- Select techniques similar in training importance to the problem.

CMS research by Reasor and Sullivan identified a wide variety of individual and group idea-generation techniques.[3] This research suggested using idea-generation techniques when making investment decisions that depend on predetermined criteria. Understanding how output flows from the strategic planning process into the option development process thus becomes important.

Reasor and Sullivan summarized the individual and group techniques that are available for developing options. They related the opportunities to various stages of the investment management process. In general, group methods are used if the acceptance of others is critical and there is enough time. Otherwise, use individual techniques.

Core Process Interactions

The four steps that make up the strategic planning and option development processes interact closely. The goals and objectives identified and the way a firm establishes performance targets influence what costs and cost drivers the firm recognizes and how it uses them. They also influence how the firm identifies alternative investment opportunities.

---

[3]Reasor and Sullivan, op. cit.

The techniques and tools a company should use depend partly on the complexity level. At any stage in the process certain information must be extracted from the strategic plan.

A single individual with direct information on all aspects of the business can use this knowledge. This person can identify the nature of the opportunity and determine what options are available. He or she then can select what investments to make and, finally, can evaluate the effectiveness of the decision. Strategic information is used but no communication of the basic strategy is required.

As an organization becomes more complex, development and communication of strategy become more critical. How a firm uses strategic information in option development depends on how it derives the information. It also depends on the extent to which defined and communicated objectives, product or service forecasts, and competitive strategies exist.

The decision makers in a small management team collectively understand the business. They either must have agreed on a strategic direction or have received it from the top manager. Only then can they develop investment options consistent with the strategy and use this information to make resource allocation decisions.

The linkage between strategic planning and option development core processes is the basis for selecting option development techniques. Proper methods vary with the level of investment or the complexity of the business.

Gaps between what is and what should be become opportunities for investment. These opportunities are the input to the option development core process. The creation of alternative capital and noncapital responses to the opportunities is the focus of option development.

Opportunities are dynamic, specific to an organization, and influenced by the complexity level of the firm. A problem for one company may not be a problem for another. Change in both the actual and desired state of a problem is constant, but problem solving requires preconditions such as the following:

- A gap between what is and what should be.

- Awareness that a gap exists.

- Both the motivation and the desire to reduce the existing gap.

- The ability to estimate (measure) the size of the gap.

- The skills and resources in place (or obtainable) to close the gap.

An organization faces well-structured, semistructured, and ill-structured problems. Standard procedures are adequate for well-structured problems because the necessary information is available. Semistructured problems involve more uncertainty about how to close the identified gap. When no obvious alternatives exist for reducing the gap between what is and what should be, you have an ill-structured problem. Most problems identified as part of the strategic planning process, particularly in higher levels of organizational or investment complexity, are in this group. You must use creative problem-solving techniques to attack these problems.

A classic problem-solving model,[4] presented in Exhibit 4-2, clarifies the boundaries between the investment core processes in the matrix. The option development process in investment management corresponds to the design phase of problem solving. Strategic planning is the intelligence phase. This model depicts the linkages among the basic investment management core processes. For example, an identified problem must have a tentative solution before there can be implementation.

> *Problems in the market mean a company needs to improve product quality. Because of the problems, the firm examines solution options. It may reformulate the product or buy a different type of production equipment. If the acquisition of new equipment is the solution, the firm must analyze competing equipment and make a selection. Finally, the company makes the acquisition. It then can track the effectiveness of the choice.*

Relationship Between Strategic Planning and Option Development

A premise of the investment management matrix is that there must be a balanced linkage among the core processes and the complexity level of the company or investment. To illustrate, we examine the relationship between strategic planning and option development for selected complexity levels.

In a level one organization the decision maker has direct knowledge of all aspects of the business. Strategic

---

[4]Modified from A.B. VanGundy, *Creative Problem Solving: A Guide for Trainers and Management,* Quorum Books, Westport, Conn., 1987, abstracted from CAM-I CMS option research by Reasor and Sullivan.

Exhibit 4-2. A PROBLEM-SOLVING PROCESS MODEL

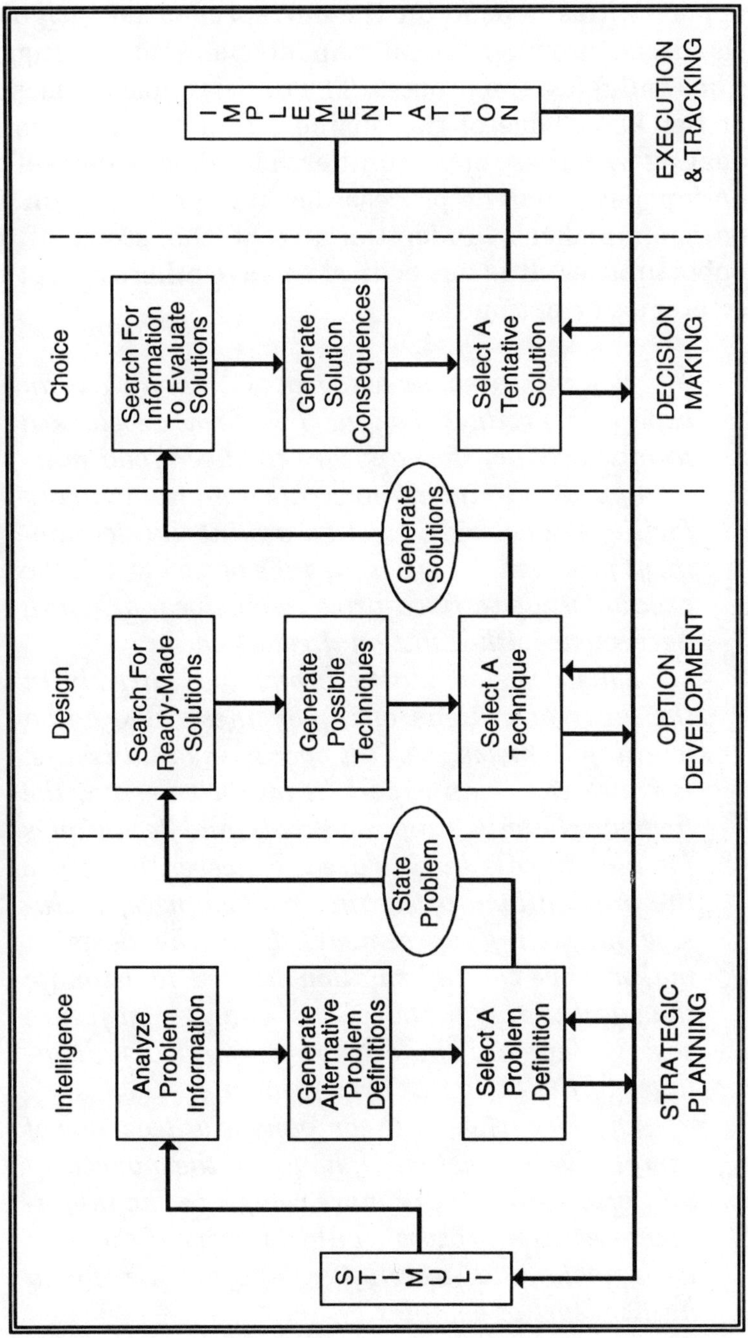

opportunities depend on the entrepreneurial insight of
the decision maker. Legal mandates and ad hoc suggestions influence the process. The decision maker uses his
or her knowledge of the business to define options for
dealing with these opportunities. The effectiveness of the
option development process depends primarily on the
decision maker's understanding of the scope of the
opportunities. It is not critical to have others accept the
strategies or options.

> *The entrepreneur who runs Company Y is an*
> *expert in product design. The firm develops a*
> *unique product that appears to have broad mar-*
> *ket appeal. Financing to create a manufacturing*
> *facility is available through a minority develop-*
> *ment program. There is also the option to sell the*
> *product under a fixed-price, exclusive marketing*
> *agreement with a national retail chain.*
>
> *This decision maker is involved directly in*
> *the daily operations of the business. She has a*
> *working knowledge of all operations and issues.*
> *Because she is an expert in product design, the*
> *firm needs only stage one tools and techniques*
> *for investments in this area. However, what are*
> *the implications of signing a fixed-price, exclu-*
> *sive marketing agreement? Does the decision*
> *maker have the information needed to estimate*
> *the effect of raw material cost changes on future*
> *costs? What are the advantages and disadvan-*
> *tages of the exclusive arrangement?*
>
> *On the surface this company is at level one of*
> *complexity. Realistically, however, the marketing*
> *and pricing areas are more complex. The invest-*
> *ment decision process would improve if the firm*
> *used tools and techniques appropriate for a*
> *higher level of complexity.*

As illustrated, even simple organizations usually require information from a group of people. They use this information to develop strategic choices for major investment decisions. In a level two firm, communication that uses the collective knowledge of this group is essential. The strategic plan often leads to an investment strategy that focuses on cash flows and total budgets (financial measures) when ranking investment projects. There is input from multiple disciplines.

Company Y may collect explicit information on the cost of making and distributing its product. It also may gather information on the activities that add to these costs. Assume the initial strategic choice of the Company Y decision maker is to use an exclusive marketing arrangement. A decision team then can identify options that increase the benefits of this strategic approach. For example, the team might consider factors such as the length of the contract and the price agreement. They may study any factors that would cause price changes and then determine if the agreement should cover only the original product.

As a company grows in complexity, management recognizes that it cannot achieve all strategic goals but must select the best strategies. The top decision maker no longer has personal knowledge of all functions and areas. A team approach to investment management is essential.

The firm establishes and communicates corporate strategies, which define objectives, scope, and purpose. Business strategies identify opportunities within the context of profitability, growth, and market share goals. Input from the cost management system helps identify costs and causes of costs. This input is the starting point for identifying alternative opportunities. For major opportunities, interdisciplinary input and acceptance are essential.

Improvements in a company's investment management process take place when there is a balanced linkage between the core process steps and the complexity level.

Company X has grown because of wide demand for its unique product. Profits have not kept pace, and the company is experiencing cash flow problems. Examination shows that production facilities (the decision maker's area of expertise) are state of the art. However, the decision maker receives only limited input from experts in marketing and finance when developing strategy and examining options. The cost management system is the financial system created soon after the company started. It provides little information on the cost of producing or distributing the product.

The firm is operating as a level one company, even though it has become at least level three in complexity. Improvements in the investment management process tools will have positive effects.

In a complex company a functional structure stratified by discipline, region, or business type provides input for the investment process. The company's strategy should be linked to performance measures, targets, goals, and objectives that benefit from the inputs of multifunctional teams.

The option development should be tied directly to strategy. Process improvement is likely as the company eliminates functional silos and moves to a multidiscipline approach. Ultimately an integrated organization develops a seamless investment management process.

Summary

There is a logical link between the core processes of strategic planning and option development. The techniques and tools used depend partially on the complexity level of the company. Corporate and business strategy influence the cost drivers (causes of cost) identified and the development of alternatives.

Opportunities for investment are created when there are gaps between what is and what should be. Usually problems are ill structured as they move from strategic development to the option development process. At this point, it is necessary to redefine and analyze the problems and then generate solution ideas. A variety of idea-generation techniques may be useful.

Chapter 5

Investment Management Decision Tools

The decision-making core process includes three investment management steps. The investment evaluation step is the focus of this chapter. Descriptions and examples of investment analysis methodology illustrate the types of tools that are useful when a firm reaches a specific level of the investment management matrix.

The three steps within the decision-making core process interact. The techniques used in risk analysis and the investment selection process relate to the way the company uses investment evaluation tools. There are also linkages to the levels reached in the other core processes. Opportunities for improvement exist when the core process steps don't balance. At any level in the matrix the firm extracts certain information from the strategic plan. Business objectives, product or service forecasts, and competitive strategies influence how it uses this information in investment evaluation. The sophistication of a firm's "cause of cost" identification and performance targets also directly influences investment analysis.

A firm makes a strategic decision to emphasize liquidity. This decision causes decision makers to focus on the investments that provide rapid positive cash flows. Long-term investments that offer high returns but lengthy cash flows would not be considered favorably by the decision makers.

A group of related projects make up a portfolio. Ideally, a firm selects an investment portfolio after taking the following actions:

- Determine that the projects meet the strategic objectives of the firm.

- Define the costs and benefits of the entire portfolio.

- Assess the risks of the individual projects as well as the risks of the total portfolio.

- Maximize the project benefits within existing resource constraints.

The firm may meet these criteria at any level of the matrix. When an organization is very complex, top decision makers have less direct knowledge of all aspects of the business operations. This factor makes communication and the use of sophisticated investment analysis tools important.

Matching Matrix Levels with Investment Evaluation Tools

Management instinct is a critical part of the investment evaluation process. No matter how sophisticated the analytical technique, judgment and feel are key parts of investment decision making. The manager who knows the business or is close to the process often is able to make sound evaluations without formal analysis. This process is particularly likely if the company (or part of a company) is relatively small and has understood, though informal, strategic goals.

At this stage, a firm invests when financial resources are available. Management instinct, based on direct knowledge of the business, suggests when there is a need for investment.

In another form, the manager may predetermine the level of investment spending and base decisions on the remaining budget. At level one, there is little formal strategic reasoning behind the decisions. Explicit option development and specialized tracking of investment results are rare. The decision maker performs all these process steps informally.

> *The owner/manager of Company Z does not buy new equipment unless he can pay cash. When money is available the decision about which equipment to buy depends on the owner/manager's long experience in the business. He also factors in his direct knowledge of any problems in the production area. An implicit, but perhaps not explicitly communicated, strategy is not to borrow money. This strategic goal directly limits the options available for dealing with opportunities. Formal methods for evaluating which options to consider and for selecting which equipment to buy are unnecessary because of the expertise of the owner/manager.*

Knowledge of the business remains an important part of the investment management process at all levels of complexity. All process steps, such as investment evaluation, are additive. You append new skills while retaining prior skills. As the firm or investment decision evolves to a higher level of complexity, investment analysis requires better communication. You also need different tools to select the investment portfolio.

An Illustrative Scenario

Problems develop when you use lower-level tools than the investment decision requires. The complexity of the investment or the complexity of the firm may cause this result. Consider the following dialogue between two employees in Company A. This firm has grown and needs a decision-making team. Sue says:

> *"Joe, I have this worn-out piece of production equipment that can no longer produce a consistent quality product. We need to replace that piece of equipment. I can get an updated model of the same machine for $400,000."*

The need to make the replacement seems obvious. The evaluation—that replacement with a newer model will solve the quality problem—may be a simple "seat-of-the-pants" judgment. A key issue is whether replacement is the proper option. Has the firm considered substituting a different type of equipment or equipment with more capacity? If there is balance between the investment step and the complexity level of the organization, Joe may reply:

> *"It sounds reasonable, Sue. After all, you are the production expert, and we have made product quality a key goal. Have you checked with Chris to be sure this machine has enough capacity to help serve that developing new market? Also, will this machine make that gadget Terry invented and is soon going to produce? Because of the cost of this new machine, it would be a good idea to*

write up your suggestions. Use that new form we created. Bring it to the meeting on Tuesday so the group can review the proposal. I will get to work on how we can finance this investment."

Several factors must be considered. The company has a somewhat formalized process for making the investment decision. Management is aware that money must be available or become available before making an investment. Desirable investments may not be possible if the firm cannot get the resources. The managerial instinct—that the firm needs to invest but also must have money available—is integral to the evaluation process at all complexity levels.

If Company A were still using level one decision-making processes, after Sue proposed the $400,000 investment Joe might respond:

"Sue, after we discussed the new production machine, I looked at our recent cash flow. The $400,000 you need to replace the old production equipment is available. Go ahead and make the acquisition."

Even though the cash is available, there is no basis for determining whether getting the new machine is the proper use for this money. The decision maker also didn't consider whether the new machine would meet the needs that would be created by a new product or new market.

Advance recognition that investments are necessary may result in the creation of a budget for groups of project types. The budget is only a planning tool, however. By itself, a budget does nothing to help assure managers that investment options are being evaluated properly.

For example, Joe says:

> *"Sue, my budget shows that we can spend $2,000,000 this year for new equipment. I have had requests to spend only $300,000 so far, so go ahead with that $400,000 machine. You might as well do it now before someone else does."*

How does Joe know this investment is the right one? Is it consistent with the strategic needs of the company? Does it really represent the best solution to the perceived problem?

Our premise is that the firm evolves to new processes and tools only when necessary. The cause is the importance of the investment decision or the organizational complexity of the company. Most firms understand the problems of taking a crisis approach to management decisions. They recognize the dangers of simply spending when dollars are available and the difficulties with a "who asked first?" philosophy. These firms move quickly beyond this level, at least in the investment evaluation step.

Investment Evaluation Through the Complexity Levels

As the business grows it adopts formal procedures and methods of evaluation. When it reaches a level three organization structure it probably has the following procedures:

- Standard forms for investment proposals.

- Approvals, at one or more levels of the organization, before an individual makes an expenditure; the size of the investment often determines the approval level necessary.

- Procedures for reviewing investment proposals and the assumptions behind them.

- Lists of factors to consider when developing an investment proposal.

The investment evaluation process is more formal because it has to be. If requests for investment dollars regularly exceed the available funds, company management quickly determines it needs techniques for comparing alternatives and choosing investments. At a minimum, this choice requires an approval process and decision makers with information in common about proposed investments.

In some situations information presented in a standardized format may be enough. By combining it with management judgment and knowledge of the business, the firm can evaluate investment proposals effectively. However, simple decision models such as payback are likely to be part of the investment evaluation effort.

As the need for more formalized decision models becomes obvious, transition in the investment analysis techniques continues. A level three organization can use traditional, single-measure financial decision models effectively. Examples of such models include return on net assets (RONA), net present value (NPV), and internal rate of return (IRR). The use of single-measure financial models means. that the company does some strategic planning and has an option development process.

The NPV method requires a hurdle rate. Having this rate means that the company understands the importance of cash flows and that it recognizes the need for priorities in considering capital budget requests. Support disciplines help complete the analysis. NPV is used to compare alternatives generated throughout the firm.

It is useless to spend time and energy on NPV analysis if the firm follows a "first request when money is available" approval process. The firm would not benefit from a formal analysis because there would be no linkage of the investment process steps. In other words, the analysis would waste company resources.

As the company or the investment decision becomes more complex, firms develop and use multiple decision criteria models. In a level four organization, it is essential that techniques link explicitly to corporate strategy, consider risk, and measure performance value. Ultimately, the company may develop tools and procedures that permit continuous improvement within the context of the overall management system.

The Tools Progression

Several tools are useful in the later stages of the investment evaluation complexity evolution. The tools selected for investment evaluation should be consistent with the complexity level of the organization or the investment. A balanced linkage among the core processes is necessary for the company to realize the benefits of using more complex evaluation tools.

Exhibit 5-1 summarizes the model groupings, the criteria used in the model, and the types of projects. Consider uncertainty or risk when applying any evaluation models. Risk analysis is discussed in Chapter 6.

You can use manual approaches or spreadsheet programs with each investment model. Computer-based decision support systems also may help in analyzing investment opportunities. These systems, such as knowledge-based expert systems (artificial intelligence), are just emerging as analysis tools.

A variety of other issues are associated with the use of any tool for investment analysis. They include risk

Exhibit 5-1. THE MODEL GROUPINGS

Type of Model	Criteria Used	Project or Program Makeup
Traditional model	One (financial)	Single project or difference between two mutually exclusive options
Multiple attribute decision model	Many quantitative and qualitative	Several mutually exclusive projects (taken one at a time)
Portfolio	One (financial)	Groups of related projects
Combination	Many quantitative and qualitative	Groups of related projects

management, accounting for capital decay, abandonment (disinvestment) options, and continuous project evaluation. We briefly discuss these techniques in Chapter 7. Research studies sponsored by the CMS program of CAM-I detail the methodologies associated with these techniques.

Single Criterion Investment Models

Single criterion (traditional financial) models based on financial measurements are common in investment analysis. They are easy to apply and relate logically to traditional management accounting procedures. These models are used to analyze individual projects or to evaluate the differences between mutually exclusive projects.

The techniques typically result in the calculation of a specific numerical result that is compared to a single quantitative criterion—normally a financial measure.

Examples include net present value, internal rate of return, and return on investment (ROI). You may use multiple iterations of the single criterion model as part of the project evaluation process. Some firms now use single criterion models based on (shareholder) value. Often firms maintain standard, single criterion models or combinations of models as spreadsheet templates and use these models throughout the company.

The advantages and disadvantages of single criterion techniques are widely documented. Many companies are using these methods. The extensive work done with these models is one reason many firms have progressed further in this step than they have in the other core steps. Unbalanced linkages are likely to exist, which means there are opportunities to improve the investment decision process.

Single criterion financial models are useful, but they have some significant limitations. These limitations are particularly important in complex organizations that include several layers of management. Two issues are of particular concern.

- Strategic investments in new or emerging technologies often require a long period of investment (cash outflows) before the firm realizes significant cash benefits. Investment analysis methods that focus on quick payback or that heavily discount future cash flows may create bias against these strategic investments.

- Evaluation techniques that do not consider traditional nonfinancial strategies, such as quality improvement, also may penalize strategic technological investments.

These perceived limitations suggest that complex companies should use multiple criteria decision models for investment management. This type of model also can provide the basic framework for the development of expert decision support systems.

Research on the strengths and limitations of single criterion systems continues. Study of methods of converting nonfinancial criteria into financial measurements also continues.

Tools for Handling Multiple Criteria

Multiple Criteria Decision Models

Linking investment decisions to strategic plans requires balancing several distinct criteria. The criteria include those used for assessing value added, the *financial perspective,* and internal and external results, the *customer perspective.* They also include functional criteria, the *business process perspective,* and business improvement, the *learning/innovation perspective.* Multiple criteria models allow decision makers to assess financial, nonfinancial quantitative, and qualitative factors simultaneously.

For many investment decisions, such as those for automated manufacturing systems, traditional single-attribute measures of financial worth are not adequate. The company must consider nonfinancial impacts, either quantitative or qualitative. Basic multiple criteria decision models recognize that quantitative impacts may not convert easily to dollars, and often qualitative measures must be assessed subjectively.

Even simple measures of qualitative factors may be useful, however, in comparing the results of a proposed investment with other options. Consider qualitative factors explicitly in the evaluation process. They are critical to success in achieving a firm's long-term objectives.

An Illustration

Exhibit 5-2 illustrates the need to consider nonfinancial factors. It shows an influence diagram for the ICAM Company, which has a three-pronged business strategy.

1. The firm has financial goals, which appear in the "cost results" section. The investments made, the sales volume, the revenues, and the operating costs influence the cost results.

2. The firm would like to reduce the time needed to get a product to market. The "schedule results" oval represents this quantitative, nonfinancial strategy.

3. Finally, the firm wants to increase the flexibility of the factory so it can respond rapidly to changes in the market—a qualitative strategy.

The diagram uses three types of strategies, one financial, one quantitative nonfinancial, and one qualitative nonfinancial. The company can assess each of the strategies individually in its own measurement terms. The schedule months, dollars, and degree of flexibility are in different units. To balance the three performance criteria a new evaluation approach, a multiple decision criteria model, is needed.

Because there are only three criteria, the easiest way to address them is a spin-off of the "balanced scorecard."[1] The three balanced scorecard criteria are:

• A financial perspective, cost as net present value.

---

[1]The balanced scorecard is described in Robert S. Kaplan and David P. Norton, "The Balanced Scorecard—Measures That Drive Performance," *Harvard Business Review,* January-February 1992, and in CAM-I CMS program workshop and seminar materials, 9/12/90.

Exhibit 5-2. MULTIPLE CRITERIA BUSINESS STRATEGY

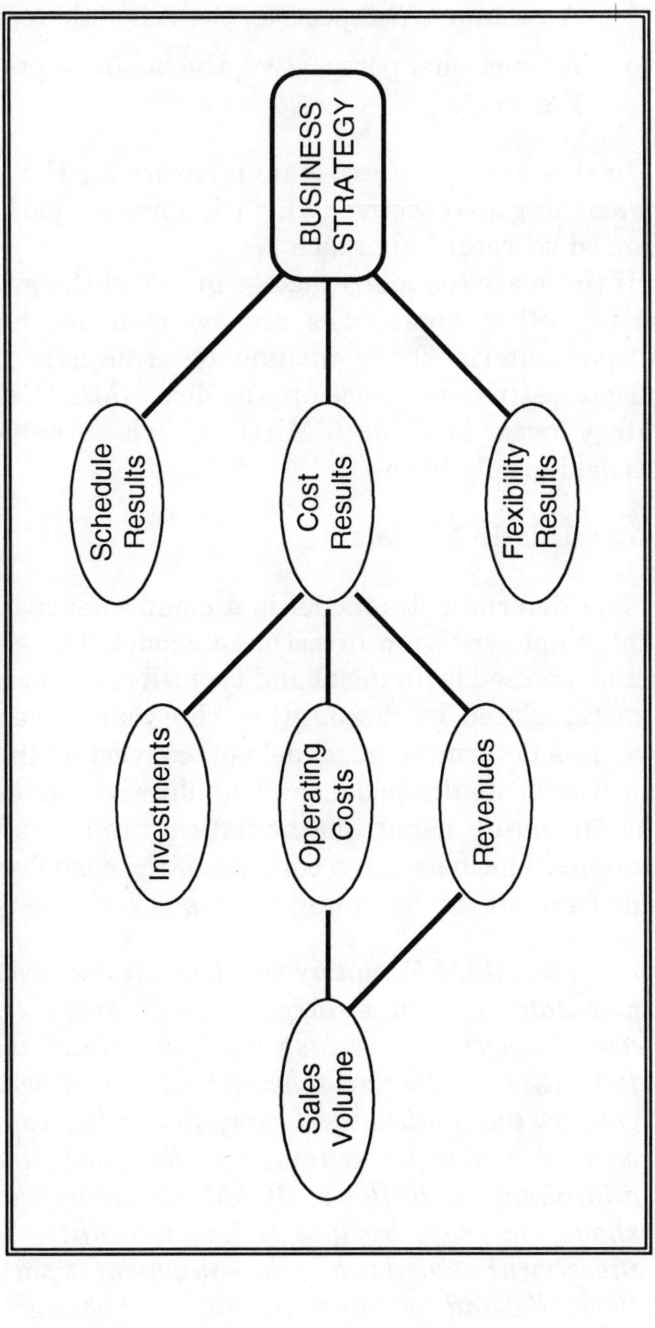

- A customer perspective, the schedule results.

- A functional perspective, the business process or flexibility.

In this example there is no measure for the innovation/learning perspective, which is another part of the balanced scorecard approach.

If there are too many factors in any of the groups or in total, other approaches are available for handling multiple criteria. They include deterministic models, multiple attribute decision models (MADMs), and strategy-based MADMs (SMADMs). These models are described briefly below.

Deterministic Models

The deterministic model is a comprehensive, traditional, single criterion investment model. The criterion most often used is financial and typically is a net present value calculated by discounting the year-by-year cash flows. In a deterministic model you convert all financial, quantitative nonfinancial, and qualitative factors to a common base, using mathematical and probability equations. This base often consists of the cash flows that result from all the foregoing factors.

The ICAM Company (see Exhibit 5-2) would calculate a "best strategic value" amount. It would determine the cash flows associated with flexibility results and schedule results. It would convert the qualitative factor, flexibility, into a cash measure by estimating the most likely additional cash flows. ICAM Company sales should increase because it has flexibility. The investment needed to buy the equipment is part of the model and considers the estimated changes in cash operating costs.

In a similar manner, you can convert schedule results into cash measures for your investments. You estimate the effects of different schedules on investment, volume, revenue, and cost.

Detailed discussion of methods for modeling qualitative, nonfinancial factors is part of the risk analysis and management research prepared by the Strategic Decisions Group, Inc. for the CMS program of CAM-I.[2] The deterministic model produces a single measurement. It lists other factor performance results as intermediate results. Deterministic models deal effectively with risk because they lend themselves to the probability analysis techniques discussed in Chapter 6. The deterministic model approach theoretically is the correct assessment approach for all strategically important investments. This decision approach, however, is difficult to model and often hard to understand. These characteristics reduce the credibility and usability of the technique as a decision tool. In addition, deterministic modeling requires a high degree of expertise, and the model itself is expensive to create. The methodology therefore generally is difficult to use unless a firm has progressed far down the evolutionary matrix.

Multiple Attribute Decision Models

The multiple attribute decision model or MADM weights individual, quantitative, nonfinancial quantitative, and qualitative criteria. The weights are based on the relative importance of the criteria to the business strategy. The company assigns a combination of weights and values to the strategic factors selected. This process is illustrated below.

---

[2]Patricia A. Evans and Paul Skov, *A Guide to Risk Analysis and Manufacturing Investments*, CAM-I, June 1990.

ICAM Company (see Exhibit 5-2) identified cost results, scheduling, and flexibility as the critical success factors for investment analysis. The company then assigned constant weights to each of the critical success factors. It calculated values individually for each option to arrive at a total score. The values were figured by comparing the actual estimate to the range of possible outputs. Finally, the calculated values were placed on a common scale, which was usually 1 to 10. Assume that ICAM assigned the following weights and values to each of the critical success factors:

	Weight	AX Value	AX Total	BX Value	BX Total
Cost	65	5	325	4	260
Flexibility	20	2	40	5	100
Scheduling	15	3	30	4	60
Total			395		420

BX has a higher total score, although it has a lower financial score (cost measure). BX would be preferred.

When trying to operationalize the MADM steps, users often have three problems.

1. It is difficult to determine the weights to assign to critical success factors.

2. The basic multiple attribute decision model does not deal effectively with risk and uncertainty.

3. Typically the number of factors must be limited, often to not more than five. Otherwise the user's ability to understand and believe the model diminishes dramatically.

The MADM model is useful for screening many options down to a small number of "best choices." The model has enough practical limitations, however, to make it difficult to use for the actual selection of the investment. Consideration of these and other aspects of the MADM model are beyond the scope of this guide.

Strategy-based Multiple Attribute Decision Models

Strategy-based MADMs (SMADMs)[3] are hybrids of the deterministic and multiple attribute decision models. In the SMADM the values are the actual estimates for each unit, while the weight is a financial conversion factor.

A sequence of operating decisions commits resources across lines of business. This commitment is part of the effort to reach the goals set by strategic planning. Strategic plans are more effective when they influence resource allocation.

The investment management process allocates a particular type of resource, capital. Today's investment decisions help strategic plans become results. To integrate strategic factors into investment management decisions, often a better link is needed between strategic planning and investment decision making, particularly in complex organizations.

The goal of any strategic investment decision should be to create value for the firm's shareholders (as well as other stakeholders). The value of the characteristics of strategically important investments often is not captured directly by traditional financial measurements. Traditional models, in general, fail to adequately quantify the

---

[3]This section is based on material developed by Sam Shafer and Steve Andreou for the investment management interest group of CAM-I.

value of strategic investments that create operating flexibility or growth opportunities.

The SMADM model captures these additional elements. It allows you to convert each of the factors to a base financial measurement, which typically is a net present value.

The NPV is a measure of the contribution of an investment to shareholder value. It requires translation of every source of project value into dollars, thus providing a common basis for comparing alternative investments. The traditional method calculates the NPV by subtracting the initial investment from the discounted stream of incremental cash flows resulting from the project.

The traditional NPV measure works well for certain types of investments but not for all investments. For example, the more unpredictable the business environment or the response of competitors, the higher the dollar value of a flexible investment. Similarly, the higher the uncertainty about the upside potential of a new product or technology, the higher the dollar value of the opportunity created by investing in a development phase project. In both cases, the project is worth more when future uncertainty is high.

To quantify the impact of uncertainty on such strategic investment decisions, you augment the "base" NPV measure. You use factors that capture the dollar value of flexibility and opportunities. For these reasons the SMADM uses a table of strategy translation factors instead of the weights assigned in the MADM. You classify investments according to their strategic characteristics and the dollar contribution of the investment, and estimate amounts using the appropriate NPV measure.

Exhibit 5-3 is an example of a SMADM for ICAM Company.

Exhibit 5-3. A SMADM FOR ICAM COMPANY

There are three critical success factors:

- Financial (net present value) must be >0; maximum is best.
- Schedule (time to start of sales) must be < 48 months; minimum is best.
- Flexibility (worst-case hours to change over production); minimum is best.

Strategy translation factors—where the base measure is current dollars:

- Finance: NPV is the same as current dollar; factor is 1.00.
- Schedule: Decision maker would pay $1,000,000 per month for improvements over 48 months.
- Flexibility: Decision maker says each hour costs enough that he or she would be willing to pay $10,000 dollars up front for each hour that the worst-case changeover could be reduced.

There are three options:

	Option 1	Option 2	Option 3
NPV @ 10%	115,000,000	125,000,000	150,000,000
Schedule	36 months	48 months	56 months
Changeover	10 hours	48 hours	11 hours

All have positive NPVs, but Option 3 exceeds the schedule gate of 48 months and is eliminated.

	Option 1			Option 2		
Factor	Raw Value	S Factor	Score	Raw Value	S Factor	Score
NPV	115,000	1	115,000	125,000	1	125,000
Schedule (48 mos.)	12	1,000	12,000	0	1,000	0
Change-over	10	-100	-1,000	48	-100	-4,800
Total			126,000			120,200

ICAM applied criteria to each of the critical success factors it identified. It placed a dollar basis on each of the three strategy translation factors and decided on a maximum acceptable schedule time for the options. Projects that require less time are more valuable. ICAM assigned a $1 million value to each month below the maximum acceptable schedule time. Using the assigned dollar values, the options can be compared directly. In this case, option 1 is better than option 2. The third option does not meet the minimum schedule criterion of less than or equal to 48 months, so it is not acceptable.

Other Models

Complex companies (level four) use functional organizational charts based on discipline, region, or business type. Investment decisions require both multifunction teams that prepare investment recommendations and extensive networking of the decision makers. A wide variety of decision tools is essential. The complexity of this process increases as the firm begins to operate globally or if it has many diverse types of businesses. Dealing with fragmented data and making trade-offs among competing business units require different decision skills.

Work continues on a variety of investment analysis approaches that will be useful for level four and level five companies. New, possibly useful tools regularly appear. For example, CMS research shows that projects selected by considering portfolios provide better overall results than individual projects selected from the same population.[4] The portfolio model is consistent with

---

[4]James M. Reeve and William G. Sullivan, *Strategic Evaluation of Interrelated Investment Projects in Manufacturing Companies*, CAM-I, 1988.

strategic planning and the current investment climate. However, portfolio investment models are time consuming and expensive to prepare and require extensive data to be effective. They are feasible only for large investments in high-risk situations with definable interdependencies between projects. Research aimed at developing simpler models is under way.

A model that considers both multiple attributes (critical success factors or criteria) and portfolios (groupings of individual projects) is conceivable. At present, however, the computer resources needed and the time and cost associated with applying a combination model limit its practical use. It works only in large, complex situations.

Summary

The discussion about the investment analysis decision step illustrates some of the tools and techniques that may be useful at later stages of the investment decision process. Investment evaluation moves from a single, knowledgeable decision maker to increasingly sophisticated and complex decision options that need the expertise of many persons. Most firms quickly adopt formalized procedures and methods.

The tools progression moves from single criterion models, such as simple net present value analysis, to multiple criteria models such as SMADMs. Movement occurs as the firm recognizes the complexity of the investment decision. A key problem is to keep the investment analysis tools in balance with the other core processes and linked to the complexity level of the organization.

Chapter 6

Risk Analysis

Risk management and analysis are integral parts of the investment management process. Events (risks) that cause the actual results to differ from the expected results are important to the investment decision process.[1]

Types of Risk

There are four types of risks that the investment management process should consider. The risk types you evaluate and how you do the analysis depend on the complexity level of your company or the investment. They also depend on how your firm uses risk evaluation tools.

1. *Economic risks* are external nontechnological risks that are part of the cost of doing business. Examples of these uncertainties include:

   • What is the future legal and regulatory environment?

---

[1]The risk discussion presented in this chapter makes extensive use of a CAM-I CMS research report, *A Guide to Risk Analysis and Management of Manufacturing Investments*, prepared by Patricia A. Evans and Paul B. Skov, June 1990.

- What will be the cost of material, labor, and capital?

- How will natural conditions and events affect the firm?

2. *Commercial risks* can affect the amount of revenues realized. These uncertainties include the following:

   - How will market size, the competition, and customer needs change?

   - What will be the effects of economic growth, changing social values, trade barriers, and politics?

3. *Technological risk* is the failure to achieve technological goals. Uncertainties in manufacturing or service technologies include many factors, such as:

   - What is the technological feasibility of the investment?

   - What is the impact of technology on product or service characteristics and performance?

   - What is the length of time until the technology becomes obsolete?

   - How compatible is the new technology with existing technologies?

4. *Implementation risk* is the failure to meet project plans due to human behavior or organizational factors. The questions below illustrate some of these uncertainties:

   - Will the efforts of people in marketing, sales, distribution, manufacturing, and engineering meet expectations?

- How will activities in information processing, research and development, and other internal management areas affect the results?

In a manufacturing environment a combination of these risks affects the value of the business. Technological, economic, and implementation risks interact with manufacturing investments to change the internal characteristics of the business. This interaction influences the characteristics of products and the performance of manufacturing systems, as well as the company's costs and capacities. Commercial risks vary with market size, the firm's market share, and product or service prices. Internal factors influence both market share and price. Business value is the result of the effects of market size, market share, costs, and prices.

Risk analysis and management appropriate for the complexity level of the company can help avoid or mitigate the effects of risk. Analysis can do the following:

- It provides a picture of the risks and returns associated with potential investments so you can balance them when reaching an investment decision.

- It provides insight into the relative importance of various risks and thus provides priorities for risk management.

- It allows you to develop risk control and monitoring measures.

Risk analysis is complex, and important risks may not be obvious. For example, it is easy to overlook the risks associated with capital decay.

Decision makers compare a new investment to the current business base. The analysis assumes an "as is" of a relatively static baseline. Realistically, the "as is" will deteriorate. Competition, machine wear, second generation technology, or some other factor alters the value of the "as is."

Customer-perceived value decay parallels capital decay. If a firm doesn't make an investment, it may lose revenue. Focusing only on cost or cost reduction is too narrow. The cost concept blocks the firm from achieving a competitive edge.

A conventional review of cost results in the following analysis:

Reducing Warranty Claims From	To	Annual Cost Savings	Investment Needed	The Cost Judgment
5%	2%	$30,000	$20,000	Do
2%	1%	10,000	20,000	Indifferent
1%	0.5%	5,000	20,000	Don't do

A model that considers value decay would recognize that the firm may lose customers if it does not make the 1% to 0.5% investment. The model would try to measure the effects of this loss on the firm.

At any level of complexity a firm may recognize and effectively account for risk. Risk also may remain unconsidered.

We illustrate this process within the framework of the investment management matrix with special emphasis on higher complexity levels. At these levels there is more likelihood of an imbalance between the risk analysis step and other core process steps. Risk analysis is a key aspect of each of the investment management processes.

- You must understand what risks are inherent in various strategy alternatives.

- You need to recognize that understanding the risks can suggest options that mitigate those risks.

- You should focus on risk analysis as a primary part of the decision analysis phase of the investment management process.

- You must relate risk management to the execution and tracking core process by focusing on critical variables.

Fundamental Risk Analysis

When a company operates at complexity level one (and perhaps level two), risk analysis is nonexistent or based solely on managerial knowledge and instinct. As awareness of the problems associated with making investment decisions develops, procedures for considering risk emerge. Firms often use a series of fundamental but isolated risk analysis techniques. Below are several examples of techniques commonly used by level three firms.

- The firm may calculate a bail-out factor.

- The firm may raise the required rate of return for risky projects.

- The firm may shorten the payback period for risky projects.

- The firm may measure the probability of project risks occurring.

- The firm may prepare a cash flow sensitivity analysis.

Often the decision analysis methods a firm uses and its risk analysis techniques are related. The literature extensively discusses and debates the advantages and disadvantages of each risk analysis method and decision analysis tool. All investment decisions involve risk, but firms would like to reduce the real or uncontrollable risks of investment. Of particular concern is the chance that the techniques identified above might lead to inappropriate choices. They also might mask the real risks of the investment option.

The process of analyzing and managing risks in capital investments is an identified knowledge void. The following section briefly develops some of the CMS research findings that focus on risk analysis procedures and models. We examine the relationship between these risk analysis techniques and multiple attribute decision analysis models.

Risk Awareness and Transition

It is difficult to assess and analyze the impact of the four risk categories (economic, commercial, technological, and implementation) on investment decisions. Investments do not deliver the expected benefits for several reasons.

- Missing or overlooking sources of project or portfolio risk may result in surprises.

- Underestimating or understating the risks associated with the investment often results in a failure to avoid or control for the effects of these risks.

- Using a "black box" approach may give unexplained results (computed data are accepted without knowing how they were arrived at). For example, tables of data might provide little information or insight into the nature of the risks or how to mitigate their effects.

Because of these difficulties, many complex companies have not moved very far through the evolutionary process in risk analysis. The techniques used for risk analysis and management vary widely. You can improve the investment management process by focusing on techniques that balance and link the risk analysis step with other core process steps. You should link at the appropriate complexity level.

CMS research[2] suggests three key factors that can help a company avoid the pitfalls identified above.

- Involve the right people in the risk analysis process.

- Match the techniques and process to the problem.

- Apply a disciplined, staged approach to risk analysis.

These factors are a critical part of most risk analysis methods.

Match the risk analysis effort, the tools, and the techniques to the investment problem. It is vital that the analysis of a small, simple investment not consume too much time and effort. However, you need to review large, complex investments carefully, to assess their risk factors.

Risk analysis can be done at several levels of sophistication and cost. Coordinate the skill levels of the

---

[2]Portions of this material are abstracted from research by Evans and Skov, op. cit.

participants with the type of investment. Balance the tools and techniques against the complexity of the potential investment.

- Simple checklists, standard models, and qualitative judgments often are enough for small, straightforward investments.

- Extensive interviews, the use of computer models, and the involvement of internal and external experts may be critical when analyzing complex investments.

Staged Decision/Risk Analysis Process

For complex organizations, the use of a three-stage process, such as that diagrammed in Exhibit 6-1,[3] can create an effective, integrated decision/risk analysis approach.

1. Reach agreement on the key issues and the reasons why they represent risk. This is the assessment phase.

2. Formulate insights on the critical risk factors. This is the development phase.

3. Develop an understanding of the effect of the risk factors. This is the evaluation phase.

Users guide the analysis team through the three-step process. Experts provide the team with information and ideas so that it can produce appropriate deliverables.

The assessment step puts the proposed investment in the perspective of the business and the firm's strategy. This phase ensures that all the important factors are

---

[3]Evans and Skov, op. cit.

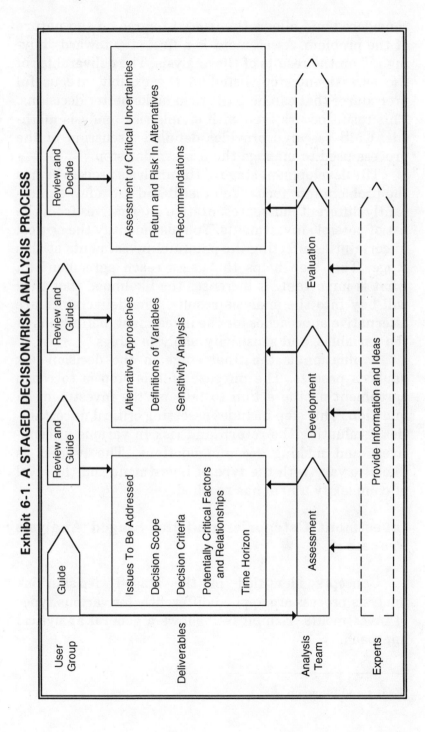

Exhibit 6-1. A STAGED DECISION/RISK ANALYSIS PROCESS

considered and allows the users to agree on the nature
of the problem. Assessment is a first step toward "buy-
ing in" on the results of the analysis. The deliverables of
the assessment step, listed in the exhibit, are useful
procedures that can help the firm make better decisions.
This result occurs even with simple risk analysis methods. CMS research provides detailed discussion of the
process used to manage the assessment step.

The development stage of the analysis process brings
the problem into focus. You distill and use a few significantly different but representative alternatives from the
list of possible investments. You also identify the critical
uncertainties affecting the potential investments at this
stage. This step helps the users reach agreement on
what is important. It increases the likelihood that they
will buy into the analysis results. The deliverables are
alternative approaches for the investment, definitions of
the variables, and sensitivity analysis tables.

Evaluation is the final stage in the decision/risk
analysis process. The purpose of this step is to reach
agreement on the action to take on the investment in
question. This step includes assessing critical uncertainties, evaluating the return and risk in various alternatives, and making recommendations. The process is
likely to vary with the type of investment and the level
of complexity a firm has reached.

Investment Categories and the Staged Analysis Process

Concepts identified in the staged decision/risk
analysis process are applied differently for various types
of investments. Exhibit 6-2[4] shows a general analytical
approach.

---

[4]Evans and Skov, op. cit.

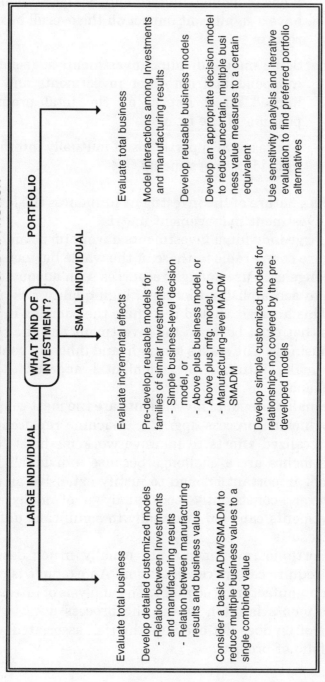

Exhibit 6-2. A GENERAL ANALYTICAL APPROACH

WHAT KIND OF INVESTMENT?

LARGE INDIVIDUAL

Evaluate total business

Develop detailed customized models
- Relation between investments and manufacturing results
- Relation between manufacturing results and business value

Consider a basic MADM/SMADM to reduce multiple business values to a single combined value

SMALL INDIVIDUAL

Evaluate incremental effects

Pre-develop reusable models for families of similar investments
- Simple business-level decision model, or
- Above plus business model, or
- Above plus mfg. model, or
- Manufacturing-level MADM/ SMADM

Develop simple customized models for relationships not covered by the pre-developed models

PORTFOLIO

Evaluate total business

Model interactions among investments and manufacturing results

Develop reusable business models

Develop an appropriate decision model to reduce uncertain, multiple business value measures to a certain equivalent

Use sensitivity analysis and iterative evaluation to find preferred portfolio alternatives

- Some individual investments are large enough to have a significant impact on the overall business return.

- Some small individual investments are relatively independent from other investments and have limited direct impact on the total profit/loss position of the firm.

- There are also portfolios of mutually interacting individual investments.

The nature of the investment influences the level on the investment management matrix.

Large individual investments have returns and risks that are comparable to those of the whole business. The challenge is to use enough resources with adequate lead time to accomplish a thorough, high-quality risk analysis. This analysis should recognize the complex interactions that exist between the investment and the rest of the business. The stakes are high, and inherent complexities make intuitive or judgmental approaches very unreliable.

Small, individual investments are the most common. They include process upgrades, machine replacements, and localized efforts to improve work methods. These investments are a challenge because individually they are not important enough to justify extensive analysis. However, consistently poor analysis of many small investments can lead eventually to significant unfavorable results.

Portfolio investments are usually major decisions that require careful consideration. An example is choosing a manufacturing strategy. The analysis of interacting investments is often weak. The process used in most firms often does not evaluate the risk associated with a portfolio of projects.

Summary

Risk management should be a continuing activity. It should begin with risk analysis and end with a specific set of plans and trigger points. These plans, when combined with the creation of contingency estimates and plans to use risk control actions and risk monitoring systems, will improve the risk management process. Several tools and techniques are useful in the process.

- Influence diagrams display relationships among decisions, uncertainties, cost drivers, and results.

- Sensitivity analysis provides insight about the relative importance of underlying risks.

- Descriptive techniques help quantify intangibles.

- Interview techniques assess expert knowledge about uncertainties.

- Probability distributions help quantify uncertainty.

- Interview techniques assess top management preferences for different types of return and risk.

- MADMs or SMADMS are effective ways to include top management preferences when evaluating investment alternatives.

Tailor the framework, people, and analytical techniques to the types of investments. Large, individual investments have a significant effect on the overall return and risk of the business. Small, individual investments have only small effects on the overall return and risk of the business. They are relatively independent of other investments under consideration. Portfolio investments are collections of multiple, interacting, individual investments. Thus the risks associated with each type are different.

Chapter 7
Execution and Tracking

The final segment of the investment management matrix is the execution and tracking core process. Once you make investment decisions, you need an implementation plan. The investment tracking system results in a monitoring system that provides critical information.

In this chapter, we focus attention on setting up an investment tracking system. The abandonment decision provides an example of the outcome of an execution and tracking function that continually evaluates investments.

Integration, Execution, and Tracking

Project implementation takes place after the decision to invest. To be effective, the investment management process needs procedures to determine how well the firm executes the investment projects. The failure to execute the investment properly or the failure to monitor performance is likely to create continuing problems. It will result in the loss of learning opportunities for the organization.

After the XYZ Company approves investment proposals, it has no procedures for monitoring investment performance. The firm does not know if the cash outflows are consistent with the estimates used to justify the project. The firm also does not require any comparison of the expected and actual results. If XYZ Company did a project review it would probably find little relationship between the expected and actual costs and benefits. It also is probable that the firm would find itself unable to determine why these differences exist.

Firms usually know who is responsible for single project investment decisions. In complex organizations, however, a wide variety of employees and functional areas have responsibility. Different persons work on the acquisition, construction, testing, and integration of major investments. As the firm changes to a more complex investment decision process, appropriate organizational structures should be in place to execute and track investment decisions efficiently and effectively. The firm must move to the appropriate level on the investment management matrix. Eventually it integrates execution and tracking, as well as the entire investment management process, into the overall management system.

A firm is unlikely to realize the benefits of advanced technology equipment unless purchase, setup, and testing are coordinated with employee education and training. Tracking whether the firm realized the benefits projected by the investment plan is an essential feature of investment management.

The investment management process is one of several parts of the company's total management system. Budgeting, performance measurement, internal control, and special project analysis are also integral parts. Coordination of these diverse elements is one key goal.

Some form of continuous or ongoing evaluation of decisions (commonly identified as post auditing) is an integral part of investment management systems. Many organizations use the evaluation step only rarely, often doing a review at a single point in time. They should maintain a balanced linkage with decision making and other core process steps. An essential part of the execution and tracking process is an investment performance tracking system. Activity accounting, technology accounting, or target costing also may be integral parts of such a system.

In practical terms, the execution and tracking step cuts across much of the investment management process. The benefit tracking system ideally would include the following steps:

- Identify the critical data elements (both cost and performance measures) that you will track for the investment.

- Assess the available cost benefit data on individual investments and portfolios of investments.

- Develop a cost benefit data validation methodology that you can use with the investment decision.

- Design a conceptual cost benefit tracking system for different types of investments.

- Test investment models by comparing actual results with cost baselines, and then analyze the differences.

- Develop procedures for responding to differences that arise, and take corrective actions.

- Design a cost benefit reporting system.

- Install the system.

- Use the feedback from the system to evaluate investment performance.

The nature of the process used to achieve these goals varies. Both the complexity level of the organization and the complexity level of the investment influence the process. If your company is using tools and processes appropriate for a lower level of complexity, you have an unbalanced process. You can improve.

At level one, most firms do little formal evaluation of investment decisions. These firms use management's knowledge of the business, supplemented by standard financial data. While appropriate for a simple company, this approach is unsatisfactory for a more complex organization. Important information is outside the direct knowledge of the decision maker. Standard financial data do not measure the costs and benefits used to justify the investment.

As a company moves to level two, firms use simple progress reports and performance measurement audits to provide the decision team with support information. A company may test whether it gained the projected cash savings. It may calculate whether it achieved the estimated rate of return. The company can use this information to make better decisions.

As a firm moves to level three, it uses more sophisticated activity analysis measures and life cycle studies to track investment decisions. The firm has a formal process for monitoring major investments continuously. This process replaces the personal knowledge found in less complex organizations or investments.

When the organization becomes complex, at level four, it needs a continuous feedback process, which is part of the firm's regular performance management. Information from many functional areas must be shared to improve the investment management process. To benefit from using sophisticated multiple selection criteria, the company needs a system to determine how and why actual results differ from expected results.

Finally, at level five, the integrated firm will have an execution and tracking system coordinated with the entire management system. Output from this evaluation process will help the company make strategic decisions, develop options, and decide on future investments.

Continuous Evaluation

Continuous evaluation should be part of the execution and tracking step. This evaluation may be formal or informal, depending on the complexity level reached.

- The process should improve the quality of future investment decisions.

- Evaluation makes it possible to start corrective procedures for a project on a real-time basis. It also may help the firm make abandonment decisions.

The most commonly mentioned purposes of on-going evaluation relate to lessons learned and process improvement. Management can profit by reviewing the results of past investment management decisions. Investment reviews provide information about prior experiences. They can highlight areas where improved techniques of forecasting, planning, and budgeting may lead to better investment decisions.

If management finds systematic bias in an individual project champion's projections, it can help make corrections. It can adjust investment decision tools, including the SMADM or an expert system, using information obtained from the monitoring process. The formality of this process and the implementation problems increase as the firm becomes more complex.

Design the monitoring program at the same time you develop the proposal for an investment. To improve the

overall quality of investment decisions, original investment proposals should include a review program. This
program identifies those variables critical to the estimated project results.

> *A manufacturing company is considering*
> *building a plant to produce corn syrup. There are*
> *problems in disposing of the waste, and sewage*
> *treatment facilities are a major part of the invest-*
> *ment. Because government regulations may*
> *change, the company may design specific checks*
> *for changes in regulations into the proposal.*
> *These checks would take place before construction*
> *starts on the sewage treatment portion of the*
> *plant.*
> *There also could be checks at specified points*
> *in the process or continuous review throughout*
> *the planning and execution stage. The audit*
> *information derived may provide data that allow*
> *the firm to adjust either the scale of the plant or*
> *the technical configuration of the disposal system.*

The higher the risk of change in a major investment
variable, the greater the need to build flexibility into the
planned outlays. It may be necessary to design multiple
specific review points into a project. These reviews will
permit the company to adjust plans to reflect a shifting
environment. A cost may be associated with this flexibility, but the higher costs may significantly reduce the
total risk associated with the investment.

Even when a firm has on-going monitoring, it may
not be cost effective to track all the cash flows associated
with a project. The firm should focus on the critical
success measures, which can be identified by means of
simulation techniques. They may include such elements
as the volume of sales, selling price, direct labor cost,

and others. The design should specify the monitoring process.

At level five, the process will link with the expert system used in the other investment steps. Management today has a unique opportunity to harness technology, to improve product and service quality, and to speed decision making. Today's technology also makes it possible to review both the tactical and strategic information continuously.

A Tracking Example

An example[1] based on a new product decision illustrates the importance of considering how actual results differ from project plans. The example shows how individual financial results may be good but the overall results may be unacceptable.

The Plan

A pet food company identifies a new product opportunity in a market with 50 million cases per year potential. The firm considers the following factors in making the investment decision:

* Market research estimated that the firm could get 20% of the market (or 10 million cases per year) at a price of $10 per case.

* Engineering estimated that the firm could build a 15 million case facility within 24 months at a cost of $80 million.

---

[1]The basic example is extracted from Gerald I. Susman, *Justifying and Tracking New Products: Measurement Continuity Between Product Life Cycle Phases*, CMS research report, September 1991.

- Manufacturing estimated that start-up costs would be $16 million and production costs, $5 per case, excluding depreciation charges.

- The brand manager's estimate of initial expenses was $20 million, with continuing advertising and marketing costs of $1 per case.

Based on these estimates the project shows the following financial results:

- Net profit of $20 million per year.

- Discounted cash flow rate of return of 16.5%, well above the firm's 12% hurdle rate.

- NPV of $36 million at a 10% discount rate.

- Break-even at six years after project authorization.

The firm makes the investment based on the project estimates.

What Happened

Through continual monitoring, the firm quickly determines that the market size estimate was too optimistic. There was a market of only 40 million cases per year for this product. The brand manager develops a new strategy that allows the firm to meet the projected financial results.

- The sales price was reduced to $9.33 from $10 per case.

- The firm doubled the initial advertising and marketing budget to $40 million, using some of the funds to distribute free samples during a major television advertising campaign.

- There was a 12-months delay in start-up because of the strategy reformulation. The delay allowed the firm to build inventory for the free sample program.

- The size of the plant investment did not change.

The changes caused the following results:

- The product achieved a 33% market share. The firm sold 12 million cases, rather than the projected 10 million cases, even with the smaller total market.

- The firm increased advertising by $0.50 a case to maintain this share. The increase offset cost savings realized from using the plant more efficiently.

- The firm earned a $20 million annual return and the financial results looked the same as planned.

- The rate of return dropped to an unacceptable 9.5%, and the NPV became negative using the original life estimates.

- If the firm could extend the project life for 15 years, the rate of return would become 15.8% and the NPV, $56.8 million.

Exhibit 7-1 provides the details about the planned and actual results. Exhibit 7-2 gives a chart of the cumulative cash flows (nondiscounted).

The Lessons

The case illustrates why a firm needs execution and tracking of investment decisions and how it can use this information to make decisions.

- The monitoring process identified a change in a critical assumption, the market size.

- The brand manager formulated a new strategy to deal with the effects of reduced market size, and the strategy met the profit target. This new strategy is the primary basis for evaluating the brand manager's performance. Unfortunately,

Exhibit 7-1. PLANNED AND ACTUAL RESULTS

	Plan	Actual
Investments		
Capital	$80 M	$80 M
Start up (20% of capital)	$16 M	$16 M
Advertising & marketing	$20 M	$40 M
Project schedule (months to		
start of full production)	24	36
Sales (M cases/year)		
Market size	50	40
Market share	20%	33%
Sales	10	12
Finances (dollars/case)		
Sales realization	$10.00	$9.33
Cost of goods (ex. depr.)	$5.00	$4.50
Advertising/marketing	$1.00	$1.50
Profit before depr. & tax	$4.00	$3.33
Total profit/loss		
($/case x cases/year)	$40 M	$40 M
Less depreciation	$10 M	$10 M
Less federal income tax	$10 M	$19 M
Net, after-tax profit	$20 M	$20 M
(DCF) rate of return	16.5%	9.5%
(if life = 15 years)		15.8%
New present value @ 10%	$36 M	-$3 M
(if life = 15 years)		$57 M

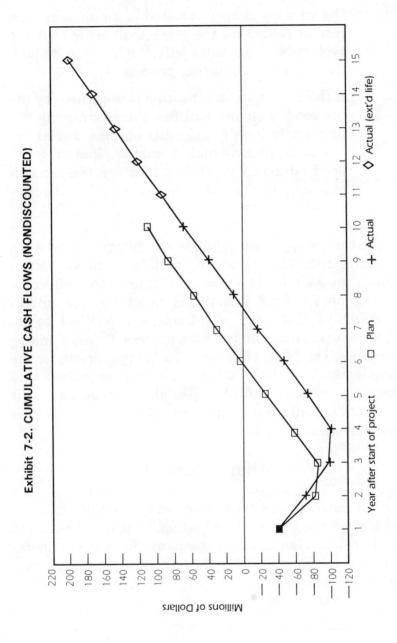

Exhibit 7-2. CUMULATIVE CASH FLOWS (NONDISCOUNTED)

the strategy change resulted in an unacceptable rate of return on the project, showing that the system did not work effectively, even though there was a monitoring process.

• If the execution and tracking process used by the pet food company had functioned properly the firm might have found other options. For example, it might have built a smaller plant or developed a different marketing strategy. If no acceptable options are available, abandon, don't reformulate.

In this example, we highlight the differences between financial reporting measures and investment performance measures. The example shows the effect of relying on financial accounting measures. An understanding of this type of difference is critical to an effective execution and tracking process. Balance among the process steps and the use of tools appropriate for the complexity level help assure that the execution and tracking process provides useful information. This information will result in more efficient and effective investment decisions.

Abandonment

An abandonment decision[2] may be the result of systematic analysis and evaluation, or it may be arrived at almost accidentally by a company. Timely and appropriate abandonment decisions have a major impact on a firm's success.

---

[2]The material in this section is based on an abandonment working paper prepared for the investment management interest group of CAM-I by Steve Andreou.

The decision to abandon an investment is similar to the original investment decision. Analysis may use the tools associated with the original decision. There are, however, differences between investment and abandonment decisions. The practical effect of these differences is often to delay the divestment decision. Some of these delay factors are:

1. The impact of an abandonment decision on people, morale, and reputation is obvious and increases the perceived importance of the decision.

2. Exit barriers related to abandonment are different from those associated with the initial investment. For instance, it may be difficult to abandon a project despite subnormal returns. There are other exit barriers.

   - Often the durable and specialized assets associated with the investment have only a small liquidation value.

   - Labor settlements may be costly.

   - Long-term purchasing or supply contracts may exist.

   - The firm may be unable to change distribution channels.

   - The business may be part of total company strategy.

   - The investment may be integral to the vertical integration of the firm.

   - The decision may affect the organization's access to the financial markets.

   - Clear information about the investment's performance may not be available.

- Managerial and emotional barriers to project elimination may exist.

- There may be government or other social barriers to eliminating the investment.

3. Decision makers often rationalize continuing or increasing an investment in hopes of saving the project rather than "pulling the plug."
4. An investment is justified originally by gathering a broad range of commitments. Abandonment decisions involve tearing down those commitments.
5. Investment proposals often start with a marketing idea. A financial discrepancy between the anticipated and actual results often causes abandonment suggestions.
6. Abandonment decisions often start at the top of the organization, not where the project originated.
7. There are differences in the post-audit process that tracks the success of the decision.

The more developed the execution and tracking system, the more likely the firm is to make rational and timely abandonment decisions.

Summary

An effective investment process must develop the necessary procedures to track selected investment projects. As a company becomes more complex, the nature of the execution and tracking process step changes. Eventually it should be integrated into the overall management system.

Making certain that all of the cost management system segments work together in a coordinated fashion is the goal. Balance is key. Frequently some or all of these elements are not properly linked. The capital decision is one area where creating a balanced linkage improves the investment management system. A company wishes to use resources to produce products or services competitive in cost, time, quality, and functionality. Investment management—the identification and evaluation of technology, equipment, people, systems, and related investment opportunities that improve performance—is a key part of the management system.

Most companies have opportunities to improve the investment management decision process they use. The investment management matrix, with its emphasis on the need to balance process steps and complexity levels, can become a valuable tool in helping a firm improve. Use only the tools necessary for an effective investment management process. It is more important to have balance across all of the process steps at the right level of complexity than to use unnecessary tools.

Bibliography

This investment management guide draws extensively on cost management research sponsored by the CAM-I CMS Program. Listed below are the sources directly used in preparing the guide. Individual research projects drew upon numerous secondary source materials.

Berliner, Callie and James A. Brimson, editors. *Cost Management for Today's Advanced Manufacturing: The CAM-I Conceptual Design*. Boston: The Harvard Business School Press, 1988.

Edwards, James B. *Capacity Cost Management*. CMS Research Report, CAM-I, 1990.

Evans, Patricia A. and Paul Skov. *A Guide to Risk Analysis and Management of Manufacturing Investments*. CMS Research Report, CAM-I, 1990.

Gerwin, Donald. *Strategies for Manufacturing Flexibility*. CMS Research Report, CAM-I, 1989.

Hamblin, David J. *The Impact of CMS on the Technological Health of the Enterprise*. CMS Research Report, CAM-I, 1989.

Kaplan, Robert S. and David P. Norton. "The Balanced Scorecard—Measures That Drive Performance." *Harvard Business Review*, January-February 1992, pp. 71-79.

Reasor, Roderick J. and William J. Sullivan. *A Conceptual Framework of Option Development Process Tools for the CAM-I CMS Investment Management Guide.* CMS Research Report, CAM-I, 1991.

Reeve, James M. and William G. Sullivan. *Strategic Evaluation of Interrelated Investment Projects in Manufacturing Companies.* CMS Research Report, CAM-I, 1988.

Sakurai, Michihara. *The Concept of Target Costing and its Effective Utilization.* CMS Research Report, CAM-I, 1987.

Shields, Michael D. and S. Mark Young. *Implementing Cost Management Systems in Advanced Manufacturing Technology Firms: Behavioral and Organizational Strategies.* CMS Research Report, CAM-I, 1988.

Sullivan, William G., James M. Reeve, and Rapinder S. Sawhney. *Strategy-Based Investment Justification for Advanced Manufacturing Technology.* CMS Research Report, CAM-I, 1989.

Susman, Gerald I. *Justifying and Tracking New Products: Measurement Continuity Between Product Life Cycle Phases.* CMS Research Report, CAM-I, 1991.

VanGundy, A.B. *Creative Problem Solving: A Guide for Trainers and Management.* Westport, Ct., Quorum Books, 1987.

For information on research projects sponsored by CMS and contained in the bibliography please contact:

Nancy Thomas
Library Services, CAM-I
1250 E. Copeland Road, Suite 500
Arlington, TX 76011

The Investment
Management Matrix

The Investment

Levels of Complexity	Core Processes	
	Strategic Planning	**Option Development**
	1. Identify goals and objectives. 2. Establish performance targets.	3. Identify costs and cost drivers. 4. Identify alternative approaches.
Level One	Bottom up list Top down mandates	Single KEY discipline defines
Level Two	Capital strategy	Multidiscipline input
Level Three	Strategic choices	Based on cost management system data
Level Four	Link/translation of strategy into performance measures, targets, goals, and objectives	Based on strategy
Level Five	Integral part of the cost management system— continuous improvement	

Management Matrix

Core Processes	
Decision Making	**Execution and Tracking**
5. Assess & analyze risks. 6. Evaluate investments. 7. Select an investment portfolio.	8. Integrate with cost management system. 9. Establish tracking system.
Based on available (budget) & "seat-of-the-pants" Investment in budget (blind faith)	Standard public data
In-depth reviews Checklists Additional approval layers Standard approval forms	Progress reports Performance measures Audits
Decision and risk analysis Decision models Customized presentations	Activity analysis & measures Life cycle records
Decision-support systems Link proposals to strategy Performance-measure value	Performance management Continuous feedback
Integral part of the cost management system— continuous improvement	

Institute of Management Accountants
Committee on Research
1992-93